Syria's Uprising and the Fracturing of the Levant

Emile Hokayem

Syria's Uprising and the Fracturing of the Levant

Emile Hokayem

IISS The International Institute for Strategic Studies

The International Institute for Strategic Studies

Arundel House | 13–15 Arundel Street | Temple Place | London | WC2R 3DX | UK

First published May 2013 by **Routledge**
4 Park Square, Milton Park, Abingdon, Oxon, OX14 4RN

for **The International Institute for Strategic Studies**
Arundel House, 13–15 Arundel Street, Temple Place, London, WC2R 3DX, UK
www.iiss.org

Simultaneously published in the USA and Canada by **Routledge**
711 Third Avenue, New York, NY 10017

Routledge is an imprint of Taylor & Francis, an Informa Business

© 2013 The International Institute for Strategic Studies

DIRECTOR-GENERAL AND CHIEF EXECUTIVE Dr John Chipman
EDITOR Dr Nicholas Redman
ASSISTANT EDITOR Nadine El-Hadi
EDITORIAL Nicholas Payne, Mona Moussavi
COVER/PRODUCTION John Buck, Kelly Verity
COVER IMAGE Syrian government troops take position in a heavily damaged area in
the old city of Aleppo in northern Syria on January 12, 2013. STR/AFP/Getty

The International Institute for Strategic Studies is an independent centre for research, information and debate on the problems of conflict, however caused, that have, or potentially have, an important military content. The Council and Staff of the Institute are international and its membership is drawn from almost 100 countries. The Institute is independent and it alone decides what activities to conduct. It owes no allegiance to any government, any group of governments or any political or other organisation. The IISS stresses rigorous research with a forward-looking policy orientation and places particular emphasis on bringing new perspectives to the strategic debate.

The Institute's publications are designed to meet the needs of a wider audience than its own membership and are available on subscription, by mail order and in good bookshops. Further details at www.iiss.org.

Printed and bound by CPI Group (UK) Ltd, Croydon, CR0 4YY

British Library Cataloguing in Publication Data
A catalogue record for this book is available from the British Library

Library of Congress Cataloging in Publication Data

ADELPHI series
ISSN 1944-5571

ADELPHI 438
ISBN 978-0-415-71738-0

Contents

ACKNOWLEDGEMENTS

The past two years have been both an emotional roller-coaster and an analytical challenge for analysts of Syria. The energy and optimism of the first months have given way to much bleaker assessments as this beautiful country faces unspeakable suffering and devastation. Yet, Syrians continue to surprise us with their resilience, cultural pride and humour – ingredients that will prove indispensable for putting their country back together.

My affinity with and understanding of Syria owes much to my many friends, acquaintances and relatives, who will remain unnamed for the moment. In these difficult moments for them and their families, my thoughts are with them.

The insights I have gleaned during my visits to Syria and neighbouring countries and constant communications with Syrians of all stripes have been complemented and refined by conversations with the superb and courageous journalists and analysts who cover the struggle. Chief among them are Nour Malas, Sarah Birke and Abigail Fielding-Smith.

I am lucky to be part of a friendly and dynamic team at the IISS–Middle East led by Mark Allworthy, who injects common sense into much of what we do. I owe special thanks to my young and talented colleagues Islam al-Tayeb, Wafa al-Sayed and Elham Fakhro. Their enthusiasm and assistance for this and many other projects have been invaluable, even as they roll their eyes at my attempts to improve their musical education.

I warmly thank Toby Dodge, Nick Redman and Nadine El-Hadi for their substantive editorial feedback and patience, and John Buck for designing the cover and the graphics. I am also grateful for John Chipman's continued trust and encouragement, and for giving me the chance to become an analyst again.

A decade ago, JRA and especially KS generously spent time and energy teaching me how to turn my endless but confused stream of thoughts and my 'French' writing style into understandable arguments and concise prose. Ellen Laipson took a risk when she gave me my first think-tank job: I thank her for the intellectual guidance and the opportunity to explore the intricacies of US policy towards the Middle East.

My closest friends from my time in Washington DC – Karim Sadjadpour, Jay Solomon and Firas Maksad – are also my most-trusted sounding board for anything related to Middle Eastern affairs. The formidable gang from the early days of *The National* in Abu Dhabi (Effie-Michelle, Sean, Patrick, Jeremy and Ross), who suffered through my zealous punditry, taught me how to be a better writer and friend.

Finally, I want to thank my rather large and always amazing family.

LIST OF ACRONYMS

AKP	Justice and Development Party (Turkey)
AQI	Al-Qaeda in Iraq
FSA	Free Syrian Army
JN	Jabhat al-Nusra
KDP	Kurdish Democratic Party (Iraq)
KNC	Kurdish National Council
KRG	Kurdish Regional Government (Iraq)
LCCs	Local Coordination Committees
MB	Muslim Brotherhood
MC	Military Council
NC	National Coalition of Syrian Revolutionary and Opposition Forces
NCC	National Coordination Committee
PKK	Kurdistan Workers' Party (Kurdish, Turkey)
PYD	Democratic Union Party (Kurdish)
SNI	Syrian National Initiative
SNC	Syrian National Council
SMC	Supreme Military Council
UNSC	United Nations Security Council

Syria's ethnic and sectarian distribution

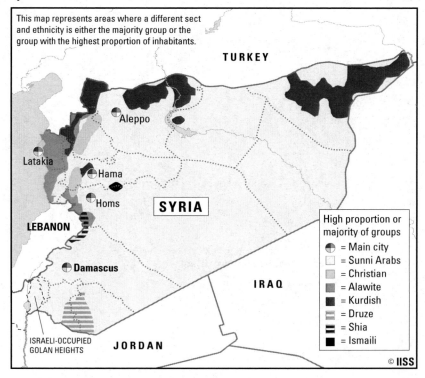

This map represents areas where a different sect and ethnicity is either the majority group or the group with the highest proportion of inhabitants.

TURKEY

Aleppo

Latakia

Hama

Homs

SYRIA

LEBANON

Damascus

IRAQ

High proportion or majority of groups
- = Main city
- = Sunni Arabs
- = Christian
- = Alawite
- = Kurdish
- = Druze
- = Shia
- = Ismaili

ISRAELI-OCCUPIED GOLAN HEIGHTS

JORDAN

© IISS

INTRODUCTION

Regardless of the fate of the House of Assad, Syria as the world has known it for the last four decades no longer exists. The unfolding and still very uncertain outcome of the uprising that started in March 2011 has put an end to over 40 years of stability under authoritarian rule. It has also unleashed powerful and antagonistic indigenous forces and dynamics that already contend to control and shape the new Syrian polity. Indeed, the country's ethnic, sectarian and political diversity, long kept in check by a minority regime through repression, co-optation and pan-Arab secular Ba'athist ideology, is asserting itself in unprecedented ways. The ability of the Assad regime to contain this tide, let alone reverse it, is limited.

Since the spring of 2011, when the instruments of control and mentality of fear that subdued society began eroding, Syria has stepped into the unknown. Its once-peaceful, upbeat revolution – an expression of profound discontent at the decay, corruption, predation and brutality of the Syrian state – has morphed into a civil war with growing sectarian undertones. Organised state violence and communal mobilisation along sectarian and ethnic lines, largely the by-product of the relentless repression of the Assad regime, have now been augmented by the perceived necessity of self-defence and the rise of violent political ideologies, including Salafi-jihadism.

Syria finds itself at the intersection of profound societal, political and strategic trends that extend across the Middle East. Indeed, the Arab world's five most critical fault lines run through Syria. The first is the breakdown of the social contract between government and society, which led to the various Arab revolts. The second is the intensifying struggle over regional dominance between Iran and several Arab states, most notably Saudi Arabia. The third is the growing Sunni-Shia divide, notably in Iraq and Lebanon, the repercussions of which are increasingly felt inside neighbouring Syria. The fourth is the rise of political Islamism and its implications for the identity of Arab states and for secular and non-Muslim groups. The final one is the balance between ethnic groups within multi-ethnic Levantine societies, whereby minorities, once marginalised by the Arab majority, seek to assert their identity. More than anywhere else, the depth and potency of these fault lines threatens Syria's social cohesion and viability as a unified state.

The already bloody struggle over Syria looks likely to be long and multifaceted as it grows in complexity and magnitude, and as sectarianism increases. At the time of writing, it still pits Assad forces against disparate rebel groups, each backed by significant segments of the population. The resilience of the Assad regime has confounded many, driving up the human, physical and societal cost of the conflict. But the demise of the regime, should it happen, would be only a chapter of an already convoluted succession of internal realignments, exacerbated by regional and international interests. The emergence of long-contained fracture lines and grievances guarantees ferocious competition between, on one hand, groups that seek to preserve their standing, interests and security and, on the other hand, groups that seek redress, retribution and power. The fragmentation and militarisation of the opposition suggests potentially violent rivalry to come over territory, resources, politics, foreign patronage and ideology, among both rebel groups and remnants of the Assad regime.

Whether the initial yearning for better political representation and governance, which inspired the original popular mobilisation and peaceful protests, can survive this cycle of violence and contribute to reconciliation within Syrian society is highly uncertain. The resilience of the population is already being tested by state erosion, urban warfare, radicalisation, rising communal violence, humanitarian dislocation, economic deprivation and very low expectations for a quick resolution. At the time of writing, the prospects for a sustainable power-sharing agreement or a settlement, which would enshrine democratic principles while protecting individual and minority rights, are indeed thin. As with other revolutions, those who inspired and spearheaded Syria's are unlikely to emerge as victors. As with most civil wars, those who will emerge empowered from the turmoil will likely be those who, having accumulated power through force but also ideological and sectarian mobilisation, will be most reluctant to cede it.

The regional and international dimensions of Syria's revolution

Syria's abrupt transformation from a significant regional player into an arena in which a multitude of local and foreign players compete will profoundly influence the future of the Levant. Historically, Syria's political importance paled in comparison to other Arab states with similar ambitions and self-image. Under Assad rule since 1970, however, Syria became a more influential regional player than its intrinsic attributes of power should have allowed. This happened by virtue of the pan-Arab Ba'athist ideology the Assad family purported to uphold, the stability it imposed onto this previously fractious polity, its manipulative and shrewd statecraft, the regional alliance it struck with Iran,

its interventions in Lebanon, Iraq and Palestine and its ambi-
tion to be an actor in crises across the Middle East. The speed
with which this accomplishment floundered is a testament to the
weak structural foundations of Syrian power under Assad rule.
The Assad regime had turned Syria's difficult geography into an
asset: it had perfected the art of helping resolve crises it initiated
or exacerbated in neighbouring countries to create the perception of power. Yet, as the regime weakens, Syria's geography is
becoming a major threat again.

In the short to medium term, Syria's neighbours, and more
broadly the allies and foes of the Assad regime, will have to
decide whether and how to promote their interests. While
many countries have already aligned with or against the Assad
regime and opted for indirect involvement, most have remained
cautious, assessing that the strategic and political costs of direct
action are considerable and currently outweigh any benefit.
However, that calculation could change in light of the rapidly
climbing humanitarian toll, destabilising contagion, the use of
chemical weapons, the direct involvement of another state, an
accidental escalation, the spread of jihadism and ethnic separat-
ism.

The importance of Syria on the Middle Eastern landscape,
coupled with an emerging power vacuum, have already turned
it into a regional battlefield. Much will depend on the repercussions of the civil war outside Syria's borders, in terms of
contagion effects, refugee flows, foul play by the Assad regime
and regional competition. At the time of writing, the Syrian crisis
has already had a greater regional and strategic impact than the
2003 US invasion of Iraq and its ensuing civil war, both in terms
of spillover and as an arena of rivalry. The Assad regime has
mobilised its allies to provide assistance and strategic depth,
while its foes have joined in an alliance aimed at bringing it
down. Small and vulnerable countries like Lebanon and Jordan
have had to balance fragile domestic politics with outside pres-

sures. Larger countries like Turkey, Saudi Arabia and Iran have come to equate their regional power with the outcome of the struggle in Syria.

In the long term, the state and strategic orientation of Syria, which borders both regional powers and fragile states, will matter greatly to the overall Middle Eastern balance of power. The region had become accustomed to a relatively assertive and Machiavellian, but largely predictable, Syria. The unfolding civil war has already shaken delicate regional relationships. Israel, for example, enjoyed a relatively stable relationship with a comparatively weak and easy to deter Syria. Adapting to a new Syria, whether fractured or strong, will require complex recalibrations by its neighbours.

An unpredictable uprising?

The fact that Syria was affected by the contagious wave of popular discontent that gripped the Arab world in 2011 came as an enormous surprise to almost everyone, Syrians and non-Syrians, policymakers and analysts alike. A relatively smooth father-to-son succession at the helm of the Syrian state in 2000, the weathering of severe foreign-policy crises in the previous decade and the internal consolidation of power had convinced many, including within the regime itself, that Assad was safe from any domestic threat. The success of the Assad regime in quashing previous internal challenges to its rule (including the 1982 destruction of the city of Hama that ended an Islamist insurrection), the strength of the *mukhabarat* security system, the lack of a unified domestic opposition and the assumed weakness of the Muslim Brotherhood also contributed to a widely-held assessment that no substantive challenge could be mounted from within.

Among Syria's friends and foes, the focus was on its regional role and ambitions: its alliance with Iran, Hizbullah and rejectionist Palestinian groups; its role in Lebanon and Iraq; its complex dance with the West; and its new relationships, especially with Turkey. The essence of the debate that animated Western and Arab officials and analysts came down to whether the regime should be isolated or engaged, to what purpose and at what cost.

As a result, Syria was rarely analysed as a complex polity. In the post-George W. Bush era, during which the costs of aggressive intervention were plainly demonstrated, the appetite of Western powers to push the Assad regime for substantive political and human rights reforms was close to nil. Rival Arab states were more concerned by Syria's strategic choices than its management of the economy or its treatment of its citizens. Steady economic growth, limited economic reforms and the appearance of growing wealth in major cities, complemented by statements of commitment and good intentions by government modernisers, created the sense that Syria was progressing. As with Egypt and Tunisia, little attention was devoted to deepening inequalities, growing corruption, the unmanaged consequences of the flawed liberalisation of the economy and the neglect of rural areas.

Syria's deteriorating internal situation arguably received less attention than was warranted, and it was certainly a difficult country to navigate. Access was restricted and granted on a preferential basis, while information and hard data were difficult to come by and often unreliable. The few researchers who had access to senior officials focused primarily on the regime's inner dynamics and regional statecraft, as they sought to influence Western policymaking. However, power often resided with inaccessible regime figures while internal struggles and debates were defined by their opacity.

Predictably then, observers did not envisage, in early 2011, that the unexpected revolutions that shook Tunisia, Egypt and Libya in the winter of 2010–11 would reach Syria. Yet, only weeks after boasting to foreign journalists that his foreign-policy credentials and personal connection to his people had immunised his authority against a popular uprising, President Bashar al-Assad found himself facing an existential challenge – greater than any faced by the House of Assad. 'If you did not see the need for reform before what happened in Egypt and in Tunisia, it is too late to do any reform,' a confident Assad told *The Wall Street Journal* in late January, asserting that Syria had already started the reforms that met popular demands.[1]

However, what started as scattered, peaceful protests against the rapacity and brutality of the state snowballed into a massive, nationwide uprising that took diverse and complex forms. The depth and nature of dissatisfaction with the regime varied widely across Syria's multiple fracture lines. If the first, rapidly contained pro-democracy demonstration in the souk of Damascus in February 2011 did not burgeon into a wider movement, the cruelty and lack of accountability of the security forces in the peripheral southern city of Deraa in dealing with schoolchildren, who had painted anti-regime slogans on walls, inflamed the country's rural areas a month later.

In a matter of weeks, it became evident that the regime had neither the willingness nor the tools to manage this crisis peacefully. Forty-two years of investment in the security forces and a mindset that prioritised family interests and regime survival over all other considerations determined the course that the regime pursued. The other Arab uprisings led regime deciders to believe that concessions would only embolden protesters, although lone voices inside the government seem to have recommended compromise. Ultimately, the regime formulated a security-heavy response and propagated a conspiracy-laden narrative alongside cosmetic and ultimately unconvincing reforms. This uncompromising strategy proved to be the regime's undoing. It was met with growing popular opposition, which quickly spread to most areas across the country, with the notable exceptions of Aleppo, its largest city and commercial centre, the capital Damascus and Alawite areas.

The fate of the House of Assad looks, at the time of writing, bleak. Its legitimacy is irrevocably undermined, its territorial hold badly contested, its resources eroding, its loyal forces overstretched and its external allies few. Still, the regime has demonstrated resilience and a capacity to adapt. It has outlived the regimes of Hosni Mubarak in Egypt and Muammar Gadhafi in Libya, two strongmen who built structures of control that were similar in intent if different in design.[2] Moreover, Assad managed to mobilise key social groups by equating his regime's survival with the security and standing of Alawite and other minorities, as well as by portraying the opposition as armed, radical, Islamist, foreign-backed and seeking to change the very fabric of Syrian society. It secured regional and international cover to check decisive external action in support of the opposition, and also obtained foreign resources, resupply and expertise to offset its shrinking means and capabilities.

Still, neither side has been able to defeat the other on the battlefield decisively. Over time, the regime shed any pretense of being a state, capable of governing and enforcing control over the population, and behaved increasingly as a militia – out of necessity but also as a reflection of a mindset that puts its survival above all else. Yet, its superior firepower has not been able to compensate for force depletion and desertions, recover lost ground and regain the trust of major segments of the population. Rebel forces, unequally equipped and organised, remain too disparate and too diverse in their loyalties, ideologies and objectives, and increasingly independent from any structured civilian leadership. As time has passed, they have asserted themselves over civilian activists thanks to superior funding, organisation and through force. The militarisation and radicalisation of many rebel groups, and the lack of decisive political control over their activities, bodes ill for a smooth transition to inclusive civilian rule.

Between them sit many Syrian citizens and key social groups as disillusioned by or opposed to Assad rule as they are fearful about the massive costs of the political transformation, the potential for chaos and state failure and the opposition's fragmentation, abuses and ideological leanings. As a result, many Syrians, primarily concerned with survival, have resorted to detachment and hedging. This is why the struggle to gain the population's support remains, first and foremost, political and psychological in nature. Military victories and setbacks are likely to matter less than the ability to maintain or gain the loyalty of key groups – namely, minorities and the middle and upper classes.

Meanwhile, options for a negotiated transition have shrunk, with the regime's intransigence and brutality and the opposition's disunity and underperformance. Intense regional and international competition has further exacerbated domestic Syrian dynamics. Ominously, the slow-motion collapse of the regime could well intensify the regionalisation of the conflict, the proliferation of weapons and the radicalisation of the opposition.

Syria's complex terrain

Syrian society is comprised of groups with widely differing grievances, interests and loyalties. The Alawite minority, from which the ruling clique hails, represents between 10 and 12% of the 22-million-strong Syrian population; the Christian community 10%; the mostly Sunni Kurdish community around 10%; the Sunni Arab majority close to 65%; Ismaili, Druze, Shia and other minorities account for the remainder.[3] Their geographic distribution adds complexity: significant minority populations cohabit with Sunnis across the country and no region is fully homogenous. While Kurds and Alawites are concentrated in the northeast and northwest respectively, there are substantial numbers spread throughout the country. Syria's main cities reflect this rich mixture, while its many small towns and rural areas, the hotbeds of the uprising, tend to be more uniform and segregated.

The Assad regime had managed to contain and manipulate this diversity through sophisticated strategies. Political activity was channeled through the Ba'ath Party, while the rest of society was apoliticised and dissent forcefully combated. Given the conservative nature of Syrian society and its sectarian demographics, secularism became an ideological instrument to justify and perpetuate Assad rule. As a way to balance the Sunni majority, the regime tied minority groups to its rule, though often in subaltern positions. It reached out to Sunni and Christian merchant elites to lock them in a bargain that secured their fortunes in exchange for loyalty. It portrayed itself as a rampart against Islamic extremism to reassure the large proportion of moderate Syrians worried about the rise of Islamism across the region. To co-opt pious Sunnis, it empowered official networks of Sunni clerics obedient to the state. It used the Ba'ath Party to build a local and national bureaucracy that was loyal to the regime and acted as a local mediator.

It is certain that not all Syrians identify themselves primarily according to religion or ethnicity. The civil war, however, has empowered sectarian and ethnic entrepreneurs to mobilise society along communalistic lines. The regime's own strategy and propaganda, and the perception that it has allied with Iran – a foreign, non-Arab power – out of sectarian affinity, as well as the involvement of Sunni Gulf powers, will facilitate this process. Syria's predisposition towards sectarian violence is amplified by its proximity to countries of similar make-up and by exposure to their troubled histories. The course and legacy of sectarian competition in Lebanon and Iraq will likely inform the two countries' behaviour towards Syria; they also provide useful analytical tools to chart Syria's communal meltdown and potential outcomes.

The rise of Islamism affects the position and preferences of minorities and non-Islamist Sunnis. Indeed, Syria's heterogeneous nature contrasts with the relative homogeneity of Egypt or Libya. In Syria, these segments of society are torn between the diminishing returns of their bargain with the Assad regime and the fear of chaos, loss of standing, retribution and Islamist governance. As fence-sitters, they expect credible guarantees and incentives to shift their loyalty, but fear of Islamism, validated for example by the fate of the Christian communities of Iraq and Egypt, makes many more inclined towards the status quo than political change.

Other fracture lines have been exposed by the crisis. The spread and vigour of the uprising has differed along regional and class lines. Rural and peripheral areas were the first to join the revolution, while the two largest cities, Aleppo and Damascus, were hit last. This can be largely explained by the government's neglect of rural areas, previously a backbone of the regime, in favour of urban-centred development. Indeed, the overall deterioration of the agricultural industry, the lack of public policies to help rural workers adapt to new market conditions, and the devastating effects and public mismanagement of a drought that affected millions of farming families from 2006–2011 are among the causes of rural discontent with the regime.

A complex set of factors explains why certain cities joined the uprising early, while others stood by the regime. Hama, where the memory of the 1982 massacre remained vivid, and Homs, the theatre of significant urban re-engineering by the regime, rose early and hard.[4] Class also played a role, as the perception among many members of the urban middle and upper classes that the revolution was led by the rural working classes or Islamists, bent on taking Syria backwards, contributed to relative apathy in certain areas. Meanwhile, urban discontent often raged in poor outer districts, where rural families settled as a result of migration – neighbourhoods in and around Damascus like Daraya. An examination of the political geography of the uprising leads to a striking conclusion: keen to hold Damascus, Assad has ended up losing Syria.

Loyalty to the regime or unwillingness to part with it can also be explained by other factors. State bureaucrats worry about their fate under a new structure of power, as do Ba'ath Party adherents; members of the much-feared security services have been implicated in massive violence and could suffer retribution; those who have benefitted from the regime's generosity and flawed economic reforms stand much to lose. But each of these groups has also experienced significant defections, out of sympathy for the revolution or out of anticipation that the regime will eventually fall. Minorities such as the Druze and the Kurds, but also tribes, have made complex calculations based on their own assessments of the regime's prospects but also on their perception of the vision, or lack thereof, of the emerging Syrian opposition.

Notes

[1] 'Interview with Syrian President Bashar al-Assad', *The Wall Street Journal*, 31 January 2011, http://online.wsj.com/article/SB10001424052748703833204576114712441122894.html.

[2] In Libya, Gadhafi purposely weakened the regular military and relied on disparate security services and tribal groups that shared little beyond loyalty to him. In Egypt, the military retained a degree of autonomy and grew estranged from the Mubarak regime, which explain its decision not to defend the autocrat. In Syria however, the army and security services remained organically linked to the regime, with key members of the ruling clique occupying senior positions. For an informed comparison of the structures of power in Egypt and Syria, see: Joshua Stacher, *Adaptable Autocrats: Regime Power in Egypt and Syria* (Palo Alto, CA: Stanford University Press, 2012).

[3] These are mainstream estimations. The demographer Youssef Courbage calculated that the size of the various minorities is actually smaller. Arab Sunnis represent 73% while minorities total 27% only: Alawites 10%; Druze, Ismailis and Shia 2.5%; Kurds 8%; and Christians 5%. Youssef Courbage, 'Ce que la démographie nous dit du conflit syrien, *Slate.fr*, 15 October 2012, http://www.slate.fr/story/62969/syrie-guerre-demographie-minorites.

[4] 'Governor Iyad Ghazal outlines his "Dream of Homs"', US Embassy Diplomatic Cable, *Wikileaks*, 1 February 2010, available at: http://dazzlepod.com/cable/10DAMASCUS93/.

CHAPTER ONE

The decay of the Syrian state

Bashar al-Assad's consolidation of power

Besides legitimacy derived from a nationalistic, confrontational and ostensibly pan-Arab foreign policy that appealed to Arab audiences, Bashar al-Assad was believed to enjoy substantive personal popularity, though measuring it in a closed and controlled society like Syria's was always a near-impossible task.

Hafez picked his son Bashar as his successor after the death of his older son Bassel in 1994 in a car accident. Many Syrians found relief in the smooth transition of power from father to son in the summer of 2000. Thought to be more in sync with his times, less rapacious, less vain and less prone to brutality than other, older Arab autocrats, Bashar al-Assad's softer and modern image became a deployable political instrument to project a sense of dynamism and openness – regardless of whether it matched the reality of Syrian politics and development.

The circumstances of his accession to the presidency in 2000 bore the hallmarks of a standard authoritarian succession: a constitutional change was rushed through to allow him to run despite being younger than the minimum age; the ruling Ba'ath Party nominated him as its only candidate; and he was confirmed as president in a hastily organised national referendum with 97% of the vote. In 2007, having weathered powerful regional storms, he was confirmed as president for another term in a referendum in which he garnered, once again, 97% of the vote and was the only candidate running.

Bashar al-Assad particularly appealed to the largely Sunni and Christian urban elite and middle class who saw him as mellower and more malleable. His father had reached the presidency from humble origins, a brutal and cunning military man of modest Alawite extraction who came to rule over the sophisticated Sunni classes of Aleppo and Damascus. In comparison, the younger Assad was thought to have been socially domesticated at least, if not totally integrated. His training as an ophthalmologist, his short stay in the United Kingdom in the mid-1990s, his proficiency in English, his much-touted interest in Internet and communication technologies and his marriage to the English-raised daughter of a surgeon from the Sunni bourgeoisie of Homs all contributed to the formation of a reformist narrative.

An additional source of sympathy among the Syrian public and abroad was the assumption that Assad's supposed reformist intentions faced systematic obstruction from within the regime, the Ba'ath Party and the state bureaucracy. In an interview early in his presidency, he alluded to these impediments: 'There are some obstacles related to the [Syrian] mentality ... The major problem that I am facing as somebody who is responsible in this country is the cadre; the efficient, trained people to do the reform, particularly the administrative reform.'[1]

The notion of an old guard protective of its interests and distrustful of the reformist instincts of the new president was given credence by the flourishing and subsequent squashing, of the 2000–01 Damascus Spring. Assad had allowed greater political space, which dissidents, mainly secular leftists and liberals, used to call for political reforms and respect for rule of law and human rights. The opening was quickly reversed: political salons were closed while many activists were repressed and jailed. This short-lived experiment in controlled political liberalisation gave rise to many interpretations as to the nature of Assad's rule, most blaming an unspecified old guard for overruling a new president seen as naïve.

The term 'old guard' itself remained conveniently abstract. To some, it referred to senior officials seen as deviating from Hafez's legacy for their benefit; to others, it suggested a cohesive group opposed to reform. The state bureaucracy was painted as recalcitrant and stagnant by government modernisers, in contrast with Assad. In the aftermath of the Syrian withdrawal from Lebanon in 2005, opposition activists involved in the Damascus Spring endorsed the Damascus Declaration, the most ambitious and broad-based statement calling for a democratic transition under the Bashar presidency. This move was seen as a provocation by a regime under foreign pressure and its signatories were harshly repressed, and arrests and intimidation of political dissidents continued to the end of the decade.[2]

This myth of the old guard kept resurfacing, even after Assad had consolidated his power. The 2005 assassination of the Lebanese Prime Minister Rafik Hariri, widely blamed on Syria, was attributed, both in Damascus and by Assad sympathisers abroad, to security chiefs operating outside Assad's knowledge. The construction of the Kibar nuclear reactor, which Israel destroyed in 2007, was said to have been imposed on Assad as his father's legacy project or by military chiefs. In the economic realm, the stalling or timidity of many reforms were blamed on vested business interests allied with regime figures, even though Assad's relatives were the primary beneficiaries of his nepotistic liberalisation policies. Few ascribed to the president responsibility for Syria's failure to sign the Association Agreement with the European Union, which had indeed been the subject of an intense debate between regime hardliners and government reformists. In retrospect, the myth of the old guard appears to have been a convenient way to deflect criticism of Assad, both internally and internationally.

Assad would certainly have had to manage and contain the political and economic ambitions of regime associates inherited from his father's rule. This was a task that began before he came to power, when Hafez started to retire and downgrade prominent security chiefs in the 1990s, such as the then army Chief of Staff Hikmat Shehabi and security stalwarts like Ali Douba. This process continued during the younger Assad's rule. The sidelining and defection of Abdel-Halim Khaddam, the regime's topmost Sunni and vice-president from 1984 until 2005, on the heels of the Hariri assassination, reflected tensions within the regime over crucial matters. Assad also relegated Bahjat Suleiman, the powerful internal intelligence chief who once served as his security mentor, and was able to assert complete control over the Ba'ath Party during its 2005 congress.

The fact that Assad inherited power rather than conquered it undoubtedly influenced how he went about affairs of the state. He did keep many of his father's aides, including: Khaddam; Mohammed Nassif, a top security official; Farouk al-Sharaa, a foreign minister and later vice-president; and many others. However, he parted with his father's habits of surrounding himself with a broad selection of loyalists and playing them off against each other, of allowing corruption within manageable limits and of divorcing security matters from business interests. Instead, Assad came to rely on a narrower clique, including his immediate family and advisers directly indebted to him. His brother Maher was put in charge of elite units, including the Republican Guard, while his brother-in-law Assef Shawkat rose through military intelligence and assumed several senior positions in the security apparatus. Cousins and other relatives were given security positions across the country, and friends and associates, not necessarily members of the Ba'ath Party, were appointed ministers, governors and ambassadors.

This concentration of power increased as the ruling family deepened its involvement in business and took advantage of economic reforms. The liberalisation of the economy created opportunities for those with access to the state's ruling clique and contributed to greater corruption and economic and social distortions. The most prominent example of the promiscuous links between the regime and commerce was the president's rapacious first cousin, Rami Makhlouf, who became the country's top businessman by obtaining fraudulent licenses, appropriating state assets and landing government contracts. Associating with him became a necessity for merchants and industrialists to develop their own businesses. Makhlouf's brother Hafez also headed the Damascus branch of the much-feared internal security apparatus.

The challenge of reform and the flawed modernisation of the economy

When he succeeded his father in 2000, Assad inherited a country with complex economic and social problems. The country's economic development was held back by lack of investment, rigid market regulations, a retrograde bureaucracy, ideological reluctance to economic liberalisation, costly energy and food subsidies, rigid currency controls and entrenched corruption. The country lacked a modern financial system, adequate regulatory and judicial bodies, and trade arrangements. Crucially, the state, bloated and deprived of foreign aid, could no longer provide enough public-sector jobs. Syria's high birth rates until the mid-1990s (55% of the population was under 24 in 2010)[3] and rising unemployment required the creation of as many as 300,000 jobs per year.[4]

Other structural constraints influenced Syria's trajectory. While it could meet the needs of its small domestic market because of the Ba'athist self-sufficiency mindset, its industrial base was ill-prepared for exports and to compete against cheaper and better-quality imports. The agricultural sector represented around 25% of gross domestic product and employed around 30% of the country's workforce, but depended on state subsidies and favourable policies. Oil production, a much-needed source of foreign currency, was hampered by sanctions and technical problems: it dropped by almost 50% from a high of around 600,000 barrels per day in 1996 to 330,000 in 2011. The impact of that decline was only partly compensated for by rising oil prices, and, as Syria imported refined petroleum products, revenues from oil exports dropped as domestic consumption rose.[5] Meanwhile, despite enormous potential, tourism remained an underdeveloped industry, hindered as it was by the negative perception of the country abroad and the impact of political instability.[6]

In his inaugural speech, Assad adopted the language of economic reform and modernisation – he even alluded to (admittedly controlled) political loosening.[7] The strategy adopted was one of gradual and controlled transition to a hybrid 'social market economy', coupled with administrative reform that would preserve aspects of the socialist system. Opening the economy and encouraging the growth of the private sector became the central focus of internal economic policy. An annual target growth rate of 6–7% was deemed essential to create enough jobs and relieve pressure on the state budget. To meet this goal, government officials estimated an annual investment requirement of US$6 billion to 7bn per year, of which the state could at best provide half, hence the recourse to private and foreign investment.[8]

This ambitious agenda was orchestrated by a small group of economic reformers close to the president led by Nibras al-Fadel and Abdallah Dardari, who rose to become deputy prime minister in charge of economic policy. Over time, the authorities opened a stock market and allowed the formation of private banks, the establishment of free zones and the founding of private universities to develop local talent. This opening up of the economy translated into greater tourism receipts and new signs of affluence in Damascus and Aleppo.[9]

However, this strategy created domestic dilemmas too. The pace and scope of reform were held hostage to bureaucratic infighting and neo-patrimonial interests. The privatisation of state companies faced ideological and interest-based obstacles, while cutting food and energy subsidies, a major fiscal expense, risked alienating the poorer classes.

Assad's economic strategy depended on the state of Syria's regional and international relations. In times of isolation and pressure, the regime felt compelled to slow or stop reforms. The government initiated discussions in 2001 to join the World Trade Organisation, but faced Western objections and internal resistance. Talks with the EU over a Trade and Association Agreement faltered in 2005 over political tensions about Lebanon, human rights and WMDs. They were later resuscitated, but stalled again due to Syrian objections. France offered technical support for administrative reform, including training of civil servants, but the cooling of relations over Lebanon interrupted this programme. It was later resumed when France re-engaged Assad in 2008. A major complication was the numerous US sanctions imposed on Syria since 2003 that restricted access to goods, services and capital. Assad was keen to loosen these from the start of the détente between Washington and Damascus in 2009.[10] Ironically, the withdrawal of Syrian forces from Lebanon created new incentives to speed up economic reforms but also aggravated corruption as regime figures who had previously preyed there had to redirect their appetite domestically.[11]

Assad fared better with his regional neighbours. While Syria faced a costly influx of Iraqi refugees from 2003, it also found a new market for Syrian goods in post-Saddam Iraq. More importantly, the political rapprochement with Turkey translated into a burgeoning of bilateral trade and investment that reached

US$2.5bn in 2010.[12] A free-trade agreement, an influx of tourists and the lifting of visas further cemented this relationship. The Syrian government had some success in attracting Gulf capital as well, through increased investment in tourism, real estate and infrastructure ventures. However, this investment did not reach the levels that were anticipated and, most importantly, it failed to create the expected number of jobs.

The decay of the state

Assad's policies eventually further distorted the economy, increased corruption and exacerbated inequalities. They ultimately, if unwittingly, created the conditions for an uprising by alienating the regime's traditional support base among the peasantry and the working classes. By failing to accompany the process of economic modernisation with a parallel political opening, while further weakening the social role of the Ba'ath Party and relying on the *mukhabarat* to control the periphery, Assad ensured that political and social tensions would find no outlet for expression and mediation. The path that Assad took under the guise of reform is what Syria experts, such as Volker Perthes, Raymond Hinnebusch and Steven Heydemann, have termed 'authoritarian upgrading'.[13] This entails the reorganisation of 'strategies of governance to adjust to new global, regional, and domestic circumstances', as Arab 'autocrats have not simply fallen back on coercion to fend off pressures for change – though repression remains a visible and potent element in the arsenal of Arab governments'.[14]

The growing affluence in urban centres contrasted with the neglect of the rural areas as state resources, failing to keep pace with population growth, were directed towards the country's main cities and infrastructure at the expense of much of the countryside.[15] The result was the visible withdrawal of the state and the degradation of social services, infrastructure and employment opportunities.[16] The government also altered its agricultural policies just as a drought hit the country in 2006, affecting the livelihoods of nearly 1.5 million Syrians and leading to the displacement of a similar number.[17] To cope with the growing pains of an expanding population, the government established government-organised non-governmental organisations (GONGOs) and increasingly allowed Islamic charities and networks to operate, so as to fill the gap left by the state and also to provide new sources of legitimacy.[18] However, these networks' provision of educational, health, social and cultural services were in no way sufficient to satisfy the needs of the population.

Importantly, while Assad asserted control over the Ba'ath Party in 2005, he also ensured that this instrument of power, which he viewed as obstructing his economic vision, was sidelined. Cuts in defence spending and new acquisition priorities (notably high-tech weapons systems) affected the standing and privileges of the military. While Hafez al-Assad has brought military officers into his inner circle, his son empowered a clique of civilian businessmen and acquaintances.

Assad's liberalisation strategy won him support across sectarian lines in the affluent business community and middle class of Aleppo and Damascus, but it also precipitated corruption and nepotism.[19] This transformation weakened the state to the benefit of the ruling clique.[20] The rise of Assad's maternal cousin Rami Makhlouf as Syria's most prominent tycoon crystallised public anger around this issue, as he came to be seen as the foremost example of nepotism. He established holding companies that connected major businessmen to most of the country's large projects, from telecommunications networks to oil production to free-zone businesses. Makhlouf's role in the economy became parasitic: belonging to his circle was a requirement to obtain state contracts, obtain banking licenses or get import permits.

Meanwhile, the liberalisation strategy advocated by Dardari came under criticism from within the state administration. In late 2009, Tayssir Raddawi, then head of the State Planning

Commission, penned a damning indictment of Dardari's performance and the results of his strategy, pointing to lower than
expected investment and job creation, as well as higher inequalities.[21]

The nature of the regime

The character and risk-taking behaviour of the Assad regime
up until the revolution was the subject of much debate. While
its authoritarianism was never in doubt, it developed ways to
depict itself, both at home and abroad, as essentially benign and
benevolent. The government seemed not to relish, or even play
up to, its status as a dangerous pariah state, on par with Iraq or
North Korea. Instead, it sought to present itself as the bulwark
against the previously endemic political instability, against the
presumed backward instincts of the population and against
Islamic radicalism. Furthermore, its viciousness and aggressive-
ness did not compare with that of Saddam Hussein, the ultimate
Arab villain. The religious freedoms enjoyed by Syrians were
well-reported, and were seen by many as remarkable.

It also found ways to justify its foreign and security policy. Its
investment in the military was legitimised by the Israeli occupation of the Golan Heights, while its stringent political and legal
control over society and individuals was portrayed as necessary
to avoid the political instability that plagued the country from
independence in 1946 to Hafez al-Assad's accession to power in
1970. Its extreme internal security structure was explained by the
ongoing state of war and the foreign pressure to which Syria was
subjected. Its foreign policy was described as the real expression
of the Arab people's opposition to Western and Israeli policies,
which other Arab states had abandoned. Even then, Syria was
eager to portray itself to foreign governments as entirely rational
and willing to adapt to regional changes, from the post-1991 Pax
Americana to the rise of Turkey. Furthermore, for domestic as
well as international audiences, the Assad regime was a known

quantity: ruthless and effective; disruptive at times but prone to accommodation; confrontational but pragmatic.

Importantly, Assad was keen to portray himself as embodying the state and preserving the pretence of its institutional functioning, even as real power moved away from institutions and into the hands of a narrow circle.

A key debate over the Assad regime relates to its sectarian nature, as it is often referred to as Alawite. Firstly, it is important to note that being Alawite is more about cultural and social behaviour than adherence to a set of religious tenets and obedience to religious hierarchies. Indeed, power in the Alawite community resides in clans rather than clerical institutions.

Secondly, the conflicted relationship that Alawites have always had with their immediate environment and even the Syrian state is also significant. The small and long disenfranchised Nusayri or Alawite community, an offshoot of Shia Islam and considered heretical by orthodox Sunnis, lived in the mountainous northwest and often worked on estates owned by Sunni landowners. They were the victims of sectarian discrimination and violence. During part of the French mandate over Syria (1920–1946), the Alawite-dominated regions of the northwest formed a distinct administrative region. The sect's fortunes improved through the political turmoil of the 1950s and 1960s, due to two key factors: the ascendancy of the Ba'ath Party and the greater role of the military in politics.[22] Ostracised Alawites had joined these two organisations in large numbers as a means to integrate socially and politically. The former's secular, pan-Arab and socialist orientation transcended Syria's divisions; the latter provided social mobility and jobs that urban elites shunned. Other minorities joined both organisations for similar reasons, but Alawites fared particularly well. After the Ba'athist Alawite military officers Salah Jadid then Hafez al-Assad seized power through coups in the 1960s, the community's dominance of the security sector became undisputed. Hafez al-Assad promoted

Alawite officers around him and gave the community a reason to back and protect his rule. To attenuate the stigma of heresy attached by Sunnis to Alawites, Assad obtained recognition of the Alawites as an offshoot of Shia Islam from senior Lebanese Shia cleric Imam Musa Sadr.

The extent to which the current Assad family espoused a sectarian world view before the uprising is difficult to pin down. Bashar al-Assad, his brother and a number of their relatives married into Sunni families. Moreover, both Assads had a number of Sunnis from the Ba'athist, military and commercial elites as close associates to their statecraft. At the same time, they continued to rely primarily on Alawite security personnel for regime security.

However, *asabiyya* (group solidarity or kinship), rather than outright and primal sectarianism, better explains family and regime dynamics and decision-making.[23] It is important to differentiate Alawite relatives and associates of the Assad family from the majority of the Alawite community. The former have indeed fared well under Assad, as scions of Alawite security chiefs became prominent, if parasitical, businessmen. Interestingly, the regime worked to normalise being Alawite by refraining from promoting Alawite identity in the public sphere, seeking instead to downplay it. In effect, it was stripped of its substance, to become solely a mark of the regime.

The question of whether the Alawite community as a whole benefitted disproportionately from four decades of Assad rule, and from tailored and discriminatory policies, is a difficult one to answer due to the limited research on this group.[24] In particular, there is lack of data on whether this community enjoyed better access to healthcare, infrastructure and other benefits. However, it is possible to argue that their access to jobs in the security sector did surpass that of other groups and that their overall conditions also improved, in ways that suggest instrumentalisation by the regime.

Firstly, its pre-Assad level of social and economic development was so low compared to other Syrian communities that it could only improve. Secondly, massive security spending was bound to benefit Alawites who joined the security apparatus in greater proportions than other sects. Thirdly, preferential access to jobs in the security services was meant to ensure loyalty to the regime. Alawites were recruited en masse in special units tasked with regime protection. After the Islamist revolt of the early 1980s, the regime encouraged Alawites to move to Damascus and other cities to create pockets of loyalists on whom they could rely. The establishment of the poor neighbourhood of Mezze 86, in the vicinity of the presidential palace, is an example of politically-driven organisation of the Syrian territory.

It was in the regime's interest to keep the Alawite community dependent on it, but also sufficiently alienated from mainstream society that it could be mobilised if needed. Economic policies that would have lifted the entire community into the middle-classes would have risked eroding its survival mentality and readiness to defend the regime.

The centrality of the security forces

Of all the instruments of Assad rule, containment and coercion through a myriad of security services ranked first. As the state's role shrank in parts of the country from 2000 onwards, the regime's reliance on the *mukhabarat* agencies increased. Under the presidencies of both Assads, external threats to Syrian national security helped justify an array of measures to keep society and dissenters in check, including very restrictive national security legislation, special courts and broad police powers. Unsurprisingly, the lifting of the four-decade-old emergency law and the reining in of the security services figured prominently among the early demands of the protesters.

Two assumptions guided the organisation of the security sector: firstly, that regime survival was its foremost objective, superseding all other national security considerations; and secondly, that viable threats to the regime could spring from within the security forces. Accordingly, the regime developed coup-proofing strategies alongside tools to monitor, contain and repress domestic threats. Among them was the creation inside every security institution of an informal hierarchy that checked the power of nominal commanders. As a result, a non-Sunni subordinate who had better regime access accompanied each Sunni officer to ascertain his loyalty.[25] It remains impossible to determine the real number and ratio of Alawites in the official security forces, but anecdotal and empirical research suggests that they were over-represented. Importantly, officers from other minorities also showed loyalty to the regime.

The security sector became an important patronage network. Jobs, benefits and favours were granted depending on loyalty rather than performance, and discriminatory promotion and demotion of officers were used to ensure loyalty. Compulsory conscription guaranteed that all Syrian men were politically moulded and tamed through their military service. The security sector became a prime provider of jobs for Alawites, recruiting them into elite units (Special Forces and the Republican Guard, as well as the 4th and 5th Divisions), which were always better equipped and battle-ready.

By 2011, the 200,000-strong military was supplemented by an array of police, interior ministry, paramilitary and Ba'ath Party forces. Around a dozen security agencies operated in parallel, the most powerful four being the Directorates of Military Intelligence, General Security, Political Security and Air Force Intelligence. Their mandates were theoretically distinct but in reality overlapped considerably. A National Security Bureau, an organ of the Ba'ath Party, and a National Security Council attached to the presidency coordinated their activities.

Hafez al-Assad, who had risen up through the ranks of the military (and intelligence services), came to power through a coup and perfected this strategy for ensuring loyalty while fostering competition between the various security agencies. He was careful to keep security barons dependent on resources he distributed and withheld, and privileges were often linked to positions to make sure retired officers could not develop independent power bases. Even then, Hafez's own brother, Rifaat, who had grown into a powerful security chief after putting down the Muslim Brotherhood insurgency of 1982, made an ultimately unsuccessful claim to the presidency in 1984. He mobilised his own Alawite-dominated Sarayat ad-Difa'a, or Defence Brigades, which escalated into a standoff with units loyal to the president. A personal meeting between the two men led to Rifaat backing down and rapidly losing power.[26]

For Bashar, who enrolled and rose up through the military after his father designated him as his successor in 1994, his relationship with the military was not as organic. His close relatives had however joined military ranks early: his brother Maher became the commander of the Republican Guard and the elite 4th Division; his brother-in-law Assef Shawkat rose to become head of military intelligence and deputy defence minister; his cousin Hafez Makhlouf headed an internal security apparatus. Many other relatives and associates occupied a variety of sensitive positions across the country, including Atef Najib who headed the Political Security branch in Deraa, the birthplace of the uprising. These appointments illustrate the nature of civil-military relations and help to explain the loyalty of the security services in Syria. This top layer of people were then supplemented by a cadre of Alawite officers like Muhammed Nassif of the powerful Alawite Kheir Beyk clan, but also Sunni associates (of both Hafez and Bashar), including the influential Tlass family.

By early 2011, as in many other Arab states, the objective conditions for an uprising had been met. Assad's policies, government mismanagement and structural challenges resulted in the decay of the Syrian state and deepened inequalities, undermining key pillars of the system that Bashar had inherited from his father. Assad had failed to develop new tools to allay Syria's economic and social dislocation and open the political arena. Even then, there was no sense of immediate danger: Assad's presumed popularity and foreign-policy credentials were seen as robust enough to prevent serious internal dissent.

Notes

[1] Quoted in: Marwan Al Kabalan, 'Bashar's reform project: Real or cosmetic?', *Gulf News*, 12 December 2003, http://gulfnews.com/news/gulf/uae/general/dr-marwan-al-kabalan-bashar-s-reform-project-real-or-cosmetic-1.373004.

[2] For an account of the Syrian opposition's travails prior to the uprising, see: Joshua Landis and Joe Pace, 'The Syrian Opposition', *The Washington Quarterly*, vol. 30, no. 1, Winter 2006–07, pp. 45–68.

[3] 'The demographic profile of Syria', UN Economic and Social Commission for Western Asia, 2010, http://www.escwa.un.org/popin/members/syria.pdf.

[4] 'Dardari insists economic reform will lead to political change', *The Daily Star*, 11 November 2004.

[5] See date from the US Energy Information Administration: http://www.eia.gov/countries/cab.cfm?fips=SY.

[6] 'Syria industry: Rethinking tourism marketing strategy', *Economist Intelligence Unit*, November 2001.

[7] For the full text of Bashar al-Assad's inaugural address, see: http://www.al-bab.com/arab/countries/syria/basharooa.htm.

[8] 'Dardari insists economic reform will lead to political change', *The Daily Star*.

[9] For an excellent overview of Syria's economic challenge on the eve of the uprising, see: Bassam Haddad, 'The Political Economy of Syria: Realities and Challenges', *Middle East Policy Journal*, June 2011.

[10] During the first days of the détente with Washington, Assad asked visiting American officials about the ways in which the complex set of US sanctions could be loosened.

[11] Caroline Donati, 'The economics of authoritarian upgrading in Syria: Liberalization and the reconfiguration of economic networks', in Steven Heydemann and Reinoud Leenders (eds.), *Middle East Authoritarianisms: Governance, Contestation and Regime Resilience in Syria and Iran* (Palo Alto, CA: Stanford University Press, 2013).

[12] 'Relations between Turkey–Syria', Turkish Ministry of Foreign Affairs, http://www.mfa.gov.tr/relations-between-turkey%E2%80%93syria.en.mfa.

[13] Volker Perthes, *Syria under Bashar al-Asad: Modernisation and the limits of change*, (Oxford: Oxford University Press for the IISS, 2004); Steven Heydemann, 'Upgrading authoritarianism in the Arab world', Brookings Analysis Paper, 2007; Raymond Hinnebusch, 'Syria:

from "authoritarian upgrading" to revolution?' *International Affairs*, vol. 88, no. 1, January 2012, pp. 95–113.

14 Heydemann, 'Upgrading authoritarianism in the Arab world'.

15 Phil Sands, 'Population surge in Syria hampers country's progress', *The National*, 6 March 2011, http://www.thenational.ae/news/world/middle-east/population-surge-in-syria-hampers-countrys-progress#full. The research of demographer Richard Cincotta on Syria's 'youth bulge' is also interesting and relevant here, as he predicted that it 'places Syria, where young adults comprise 52% of all working-age adults, at a higher level of risk of political violence than Tunisia, where that figure is 43%'. Cincotta, quoted in: Elena McGovern, 'Demography and Democracy in the Middle East', *Stimson*, http://www.stimson.org/summaries/demography-and-democracy-in-the-middle-east/. Population Action International also classified Syria in 2005 as a 'Very Young' country: http://populationaction.org/Publications2/Data_and_Maps/Shape_of_Things_to_Come/Summary.php.

16 For a sense of Syria's fiscal challenges, see: 'Syrian Arab Republic: 2009 Article IV Consultation—Staff Report; and Public Information Notice', *International Monetary Fund*, 2010,http://www.imf.org/external/pubs/ft/scr/2010/cr1086.pdf; and Figure 1.2 in Haddad, 'The Political Economy of Syria: Realities and Challenges'.

17 'Syria: Drought response faces funding shortfall', *IRIN*, 24 December 2009, http://www. irinnews.org/Report/87165/SYRIA-Drought-response-faces-funding-shortfall.

18 Thomas Pierret and Kjetil Selvik, 'Limits of authoritarian upgrading in Syria: private welfare, Islamic charities and the rise of the Zayd movement', *International Journal of Middle East Studies*, vol. 41, no. 4, November 2009, pp.595–614.

19 Syria steadily slipped in all rankings about corruption. See figures from *Transparency International*: http://cpi.transparency.org/cpi2012/results/.

20 Haddad, *Business Networks in Syria: The Political Economy of Authoritarian Resilience* (Palo Alto, CA: Stanford University Press, 2012).

21 'Hay'at takhtit al-dawla tafdah al-Dardari', *Syrian News Station*, 30 November 2009, http://sns.sy/sns/?path=news/read/6197.

22 The ultimate study of Syrian society and its political development in the twentieth century remains: Hanna Batatu, *Syria's Peasantry, the Descendants of Its Lesser Rural Notables, and Their Politics* (Princeton, NJ: Princeton University Press, 1999).

23 French political sociologist Michel Seurat expands Ibn Khaldoun's concept of *asabiyya*, applying it to the Assad regime to explain its power structure and the webs of loyalties that sustained it. Michel Seurat, *Syrie: L'Etat de barbarie* (Editions du Seuil, 1988).

24 Although the body of research on Syria's Alawite community is limited, there is the exception of the outstanding work of French political geographer Fabrice Balanche, who has charted the improvement of the Alawites' condition due to state-backed development, as

well as its relative deterioration as the state lost resources from the 1990s onwards. For more on Syria's Alawite community and its relationship with the Assad regime, the Syrian state and the Sunni majority, see: Fabrice Balanche, *La region alaouite et le pouvoir syrien* (Kathala, 2006).

25 For an insider account of the workings of the security services, see: 'Syrie: un officier superieur parle', *Le Monde Diplomatique*, 7 September 2011, http://www.monde-diplomatique.fr/carnet/2011-09-07-Syrie-un-officier-superieur-parle.

26 For a sympathetic account of Hafez al-Assad's presidency in the 1970s and 1980s, see: Patrick Seale, *Asad of Syria: The Struggle for the Middle East* (Berkeley, CA: University of California Press, 1989).

CHAPTER TWO

The uprising and the regime

In just a year, the Syrian uprising evolved from a largely peaceful and organic revolution into a full-scale sectarian civil war. New and complex dynamics have been created as forms of secular and peaceful protests have receded and given rise to a multitude of actors with divergent motivations and objectives.

The mobilisation of the largely apolitical Syrian society happened gradually and with much hesitation. While repressed and controlled, it was not as systematically brutalised or as profoundly divided as was its Iraqi counterpart under the rule of Saddam Hussein. Despite regime predation, the economy still functioned. US sanctions had not had a debilitating impact on either the state or society. The state had weakened but remained the sole coercive force, while weaponry was not widely available.

Fundamentally, Syrian citizens saw themselves as wiser, more cohesive and less sectarian than their Lebanese and Iraqi neighbours who had fought vicious civil wars. As a result, there has been difficulty across Syrian society, which had avoided the sectarian and centrifugal forces that had ripped apart Lebanon and Iraq, accepting that it could harbour parallel feelings of enmity and suffer a similar fate.

Revolutionary activists and their sympathisers have long resisted the 'civil war' label, fearing it would unfairly taint their revolution and would suggest an undue political and military equivalence between the regime and its opponents. The Assad regime too adopted another narrative: in an attempt to project the image of a state that had retained its legitimacy and functioned properly, it at first dismissed the unrest as localised and criminal in nature. As rebels captured territory and won victories, Assad was forced to acknowledge the potency and wide appeal of the uprising, eventually framing it as a massive, foreign-driven conspiracy so as to mobilise his loyalists.

More than two years into the uprising, it is however undeniable that the sustained, systematic, nationwide and violent nature of the struggle – driven by local, communal and national dynamics, and seen by every side as existential – amounts to a civil war with sectarian overtones. In the process, violence has taken myriad forms, from organised state repression and armed resistance to jihadi violence and criminal activity. Syria's societal, rural and urban fabric is being shredded, while the capacity and legitimacy of the state and its institutions, which the Assad regime abused, are eroding. The economy, vital infrastructure and housing are in ruins. Revolution and civil war are not mutually exclusive, but if non-violent forms of mobilisation persist, they no longer do so in ways that can decisively shape the struggle's dynamics and outcome.

There is no doubt that the outbreak of the civil war owes much to the regime's uncompromising crackdown and complacent political response to the initial protests. A debate continues as to whether Assad could have taken steps to avoid the escalation by holding accountable the security officials who bullied the initial protesters in Deraa in March and April 2011. Such a discussion needs to consider *asabiyya* (discussed in Chapter One) and the mindset of the regime as drivers of its response. Equipped with a rulebook that prioritised repression, inspired by past experiences of security responses and informed by the regime's self-image, it is unlikely that Assad would have taken another route.

Having failed to contain the initial revolutionary tremors yet still underestimating their potency, Assad and his security aides calculated that, in the face of massive peaceful protests, deployment of massive force was the only option – even at the risk of a civil war. The escalation was also the result of local dynamics as early demonstrators and civilians sought protection against security forces and villages, towns and communities organised preemptive communal self-defence.

The political geography of the Syrian uprising

The spread, intensity, and gradual transformation of the Syrian uprising reflect the multiple fault lines that cross Syrian society. Many pre-date the Assad regime while others stem from structural challenges and its public policy choices; all however have been exacerbated by its strategies of societal and political control. While largely accurate, the dominant narrative of an early mobilisation of rural towns and urban apathy, and of Sunni domination of the revolutionary movement, obscures important dynamics. Syrians mobilised differently depending on where they lived and on their relationship to the state, and with varying levels of organisation, persistence and success. The regime's strategies of co-optation and exclusion of various social groups played a central role in that dynamic.

An examination of the political geography of Syria, combining sociological, sectarian and political analysis, helps clarify important questions about the uprising: why, when and how some social groups mobilised and others did not; why minorities remained largely loyal to the regime or on the fence; why some cities joined the movement and others didn't; why neighbourhoods within cities rose and adjacent ones didn't; why resistance and fighting were fiercer in some areas; why opposition groups developed particular identities and strategies in specific areas; and why the regime adopted specific repressive tactics in certain places, but not others.

Rapid population growth until the mid-1990s (encouraged by Ba'athist ideology), discriminatory policies, economic and resource distortions and their related impact on the geographical distribution of the population have significantly changed the Syrian landscape since 1970. As Fabrice Balanche brilliantly details in his work on Syria, the organisation of the Syrian territory itself was deeply politicised.[1] Some regions and cities were rewarded and others punished and 'encircled' depending on their importance and their loyalty. For example, Arab tribes in the Jazeera (Syria's agricultural centre and resource basin) and in the Raqqah province benefitted from land reform and state largesse, and were used to contain Kurdish ambitions.

Tellingly, the initial protests in Damascus in February 2011, which were organised by and attracted urban intellectuals and dissidents, failed to rally sizeable numbers. The real spark came from Deraa, in the southern province of Houran, which was once a bastion of the Ba'ath Party and a prime provider of senior figures for the regime. The tribal nature of Houran partly explains why repression failed to contain popular anger. The governor and security chiefs in Deraa, who included a cousin of Assad, were seen as predatory outsiders who had humiliated residents and tortured children who had painted anti-regime slogans. Only when the demand for an honourable solution and accountability was rebuffed by a regime keen on projecting strength did the Deraa protesters call for the fall of the regime and the movement spread nationally.

Structural factors were also at work: Houran, like many peripheral regions across Syria, had once benefitted from generous agricultural and administrative policies from the central authorities. But, starting in the 1980s, demographic growth strained already dwindling state resources. Combined with competing policy priorities, this meant that the government was no longer able to maintain a significant presence and provide the same services and benefits. As a result, public investment in infrastructure and services was cut in most rural areas, affecting the livelihood and lifestyle of millions of Syrians. Over time, agricultural provision (from water supply to subsidies) was reduced, and public health and education spending could no longer meet people's needs. This situation was aggravated by the drought that started in 2006. Dozens of villages were abandoned in agricultural regions in the north and the east as hundreds of thousands of rural workers relocated to already-crumbling small towns and the poor vicinities of Damascus and Aleppo.

The coming to power of Bashar had added a new dimension. Under his guidance, a ruling clique that was contemptuous of rural classes decisively shifted economic planning and development towards urban areas, under the professed pretext of reforming the economy. Private sector and foreign investment, especially in tourism, real estate, services, banking and industry, flowed into cities. Bashar, casting himself as a modern city-dweller partly to appeal to the merchant elite, was no longer committed to the peasant and rural classes that once served as the ideological and popular backbone of the Ba'ath party. Besides the Alawite community, his new constituency was urban-based and geared toward government service, industry and services. The Ba'ath Party itself had been gutted of its ideological and administrative substance, turning into a raw instrument of patronage and coercion. Moreover, the regular military, struggling with internal dysfunction and budgetary constraints, no longer served as the primary vehicle of social prestige and mobility.

The mix of factors that set Deraa alight was also present in other regions that rose early, including the northwestern province of Idlib, which had provided numerous army recruits and

Ba'ath Party members under the rule of Hafez. There too, state decay and high unemployment among the youth led to massive discontent.

The first two large cities to have joined the popular movement were Hama and Homs, two major urban centres along the strategic Damascus-Aleppo corridor. There, massive demonstrations occurred over several months. Hama is a homogenous, conservative Sunni city scarred by the memory of the 1982 onslaught that ended a Muslim Brotherhood uprising and cost around 20,000 lives.[2] Three decades later, resentment continued to fester in the city, which remained ostracised by the central government. To the south, and surrounded by Sunni, Christian, Alawite, Shia and Ismaili towns, lies the cosmopolitan city of Homs, which had become the target of regime economic predation. Contrary to Hama, it attracted investment and benefitted from public spending on infrastructure, including in the refinery and industrial zones. But the benefits of high growth were unevenly distributed, and the perception among Homs residents was of rapacious urban engineering and a land grab of valuable real estate by regime figures (its governor was a close friend of Assad).[3] Moreover, the Alawite quarters of Homs were perceived as being favoured in terms of infrastructure, services and employment, although Alawites from Homs and its vicinity complained about neglect compared to those of the coastal areas. Unsurprisingly, therefore, the mobilisation in Homs was predominantly Sunni with considerable Christian and Ismaili participation at first, and spilled out onto the city's main square. In contrast, Alawite neighbourhoods remained loyal.

The spread of the uprising to regions along the Lebanese and Turkish borders points to other dynamics at play. Residents of Tal Kalakh and Jisr al-Shughour historically had a contentious relationship with the regime, as they ran smuggling routes, sharing the proceeds with corrupt local officials. Trafficking had however become less lucrative, which compounded resentment that had built up over state neglect. In both towns, resistance to the crackdown took on a violent nature early on as the smugglers were already armed. In the case of Tal Kalakh, the proximity of competing and better-off Alawite villages added to communal fear and sectarian bias. Along with Hama, Homs, Idlib and many Sunni villages that saw protests and massive repression early on, both towns also lie at the edge of Jabal al-Nusayriyah (the historic Alawite Mountains in the northwest of Syria).

Damascus too was affected early by the uprising, but the mobilisation there took different forms because of the spatial and social arrangement of the city. The capital had received particular attention from both Hafez and Bashar: from the former as a reward for its loyalty during political upheaval in the 1980s, and from the latter as part of his modernisation strategy.

The polarisation over the revolution was best captured by the dynamics inside the cosmopolitan city of Damascus. It was in the largely Sunni areas of Darayya and the Eastern Ghouta (notably Douma), once considered rural but now de facto absorbed into the urban sprawl of the capital, that local activists led a vigorous, and at first, peaceful revolutionary movement. These areas, plagued by poverty and underemployment, housed middle-class inhabitants and absorbed rural migrants. The conservative, middle-class neighbourhoods of Barzeh and Midan, and the poor Sunni sector of Qaaboun, also partook massively in anti-Assad demonstrations. Their residents, mostly merchants and small-business owners who sat outside regime circles, had not benefitted from government largesse or from the economic growth of the previous decade.

Meanwhile, the residents of Mezze 86, a slum housing Alawite security personnel inside Damascus, participated in largely pro-Assad rallies in mid-2011. These regime-orchestrated demonstrations enlisted bureaucrats and employees of state-owned companies and firms belonging to regime associates. They also attracted members of the middle and upper classes who had benefitted from public sector patronage and the economic liberalisation carried out by Assad. In comparison, the Christian district of Bab Touma remained mostly uninvolved, as did Druze residents.

Aleppo, Syria's largest city and commercial centre, did not mobilise in earnest until early 2012. Once cosmopolitan and vibrant, the northern metropolis became more conservative under Ba'athist rule. Long-ignored by the regime for its affinity toward the Muslim Brotherhood, starting in the mid-1990s it had benefitted from its architectural wealth that attracted tourism and from booming trade with Turkey. Balanche attributes Aleppo's relative apathy in the early stages of the revolution to two factors: the urban-rural divide, with urban-dwellers distrusting the motivations of the revolutionary peasantry, and the presence of a sizeable Kurdish population, as well as Christian and Armenian communities.[4]

The potency of regional fault lines and urban-rural divides inside Syria was illustrated by the intense criticism in peripheral areas of the relatively late mobilisation of Damascus and Aleppo. During the crackdown in Deraa and the siege of the Homs neighbourhuod of Baba Amr, their inhabitants called on the main cities to rise up in solidarity. When this did not happen, urbanites were portrayed as indecisive and unwilling to shoulder the risks and the cost of the revolution.

Regions where tribal belonging was a defining element of identity have presented a diverse picture – a sign of the way the Assad regime's multifaceted control strategies interact with Syria's complex terrain.[5] Some tribes in the Raqqah province had received, among other state benefits, land from the Ba'athist policy of land redistribution in the 1960s, and were unwilling to part with Assad. Meanwhile, tribes in the Deir Ez-Zor province, alongside the Iraqi border, proved more restless. Of course, a tribe is not a single unit (each is divided into clans and sub-clans), and the calculations and constraints of a tribal leader are complex. Tribal leaders are often local government officials or businessmen benefitting from state largesse or immunity. As a result, some sided with the regime, providing local enforcement, others embraced the uprising, thereby clashing with government troops and other tribal fighters, and a few tried to mediate local 'live and let live' agreements.[6]

The Kurdish community, primarily massed in the northeast of the country and Aleppo, proved undecided. In 2004, massive Kurdish demonstrations fuelled by decades of state abandonment and resentment over citizenship – and inspired by the rising profile of Iraq's Kurds – were brutally repressed by the government while their cause found little resonance across Syria. When the uprising broke out in 2011, Kurdish activists joined the movement, only to see the community's political representatives and elders counsel restraint. The Kurds appeared to hedge, distrustful of whether the nascent Syrian opposition would recognise their demands over power-sharing, citizenship rights and the identity of the Syrian state. The Kurdish calculation appeared as follows: were Syria to experience a devastating civil war that would result in a weak and divided state, Kurdish interests would be better served by limited involvement with the revolutionary movement and by creating facts on the ground, namely de facto autonomy as their Iraqi kin had successfully done.[7] As a result, the regime largely withdrew from Kurdish areas, counting on the escalation of tensions between Kurdish and opposition groups, and also aiming to complicate Turkey's position because of its stance towards its Kurdish population.

Another vulnerable community that adopted similar restraint was the Druze, mostly concentrated in the southern province of Suweida and Damascus. Druze elders proved unwilling to take sides, instead negotiating local deals with both the regime and the opposition. Indeed, the region of Suweida has seen the lowest number of casualties among Syrian provinces, although it borders Deraa, where fighting was most intense.[8] Meanwhile,

while the small Shia community remained loyal to Assad (partly thanks to the regime's alliance with the Lebanese Shia militant group Hizbullah), much of the tiny Ismaili sect (an offshoot of Shia Islam) joined the demonstrations.[9]

Calculations of Christian communities have been coloured by the targeting and subsequent dwindling of the Christian population in Iraq at the hands of Sunni jihadis and by the marginalisation of Egypt's Copts after the 2011 revolution. This has stirred profound fears among Syrian Christians, who valued the religious freedoms ensured by the Assad regime and its minority character. It was assumed that a Sunni Islamist government would reverse such liberties, undo their more liberal way of life and relegate Christians in politics and business. As a result, many Christian clerics and community leaders have maintained their support for Assad in public and private.

Unsurprisingly, the uprising found no discernible resonance in the Alawite region of Jabal al-Nusayriyah. The fortunes of the Alawite community considerably improved during Assad rule, generating loyalty and dependence. Dissent persisted however: prior to the uprising, the Syrian opposition had included prominent Alawite figures. Furthermore, some Alawites were active in the protest movement from 2011, including writer Samar Yazbek, prominent dissident Abdelaziz al-Khair, human-rights advocate Mazen Darwish and long-time oppositionist-in-exile Mounzer Makhous. However, as of early 2013, there were no defections from senior Alawite regime figures. Faced with the prospect of sectarian retribution – a sentiment cultivated by the regime to mobilise Alawites in its defence – a sense of fear mixed with urgency descended on this community. Accordingly, Alawite villages on the outer edge of Jabal al-Nusayriyah and in the vicinity of Homs saw a massive deployment of communal self-defence units. The Alawite-dominated coastal city of Latakia experienced some unrest, but tellingly in its poor Sunni neighbourhoods and in its Palestinian refugee camp.

Several conclusions emerge from this analysis of the political geography of the initial stages of the uprising. The revolution started as overwhelmingly Sunni, largely peripheral and mostly lower- and middle-class. Local conditions and grievances fuelled the uprising as much as an idealistic revolutionary ethos did. Clearly defined Islamist motivations (as opposed to Sunni communal resentment) seem not to have been among the original underlying reasons for the unrest. While sectarian slogans were wielded in some regions where several communities coexisted, they were absent in many other regions and spread only as fighting intensified, fostering radicalisation and sectarianism.

This analysis must also include other factors. Due to higher birth rates, the size of the Sunni community relative to more affluent communities has increased, and this had an impact on the Assad regime's control strategy. It also affected the calculations of minorities, who were increasingly fearful of living in a 'Sea of Sunnis'.[10]

However, concluding that the uprising began as overwhelmingly Sunni should not lead to a view that all Sunnis rose up, nor that the revolutionary dynamic was primarily sectarian. Often shunned by their own sects, non-Sunni revolutionary activists travelled to other areas to protest and organise. This was especially the case in Damascus and Homs. Political, religious and business leaders of minorities, arguably backed by the majority of their members, refused to take on the costs of an uncertain confrontation with a regime that ensured freedom of religion (while denying all political freedoms), sometimes gave them a role in the running of the state and ostensibly kept Sunni radicalism in check.

Importantly, many Sunnis continued to support the Assad regime well into the revolution, for various reasons. Some did so out of loyalty and self-interest: the regime provided jobs to many Sunnis in the state bureaucracy and military and worked with Sunni businessmen in its economic dealings. The Ba'ath

Party also counted many Sunnis among its members at all levels of command, although it had become increasingly marginal in running the state. Others, mindful of Syria's long history of pre-Assad political instability and fearing the unknown, were attached to the idea of the state and political continuity. Others still, from urban communities, feared the prospect of an Islamist government that would redefine Syria's identity. Finally, many adhered to Assad's foreign policy and derived pride from Syria's steadfastness against Israeli and Western policies.

The regime's response and resilience

The Assad regime has demonstrated considerable strength and tenacity. At several points in the conflict, notably in July and December 2012, a sense of momentum born of rebel successes engendered talk of an imminent endgame. However, defying regular predictions of a quick collapse, the regime had survived the various mutations of the conflict into 2013, and demonstrated extraordinary cohesion. It has been able to withstand a lot: while senior figures defected or were assassinated, it showed little sign of an impending internal unravelling or coup; while challenged in every major city, it had lost none; while having been booted out of much of the countryside, it remained in control of key infrastructure and roads; and while its regular military took heavy casualties, its elite units remained loyal and battle-ready. Furthermore, most state bureaucrats, including judges, diplomats and civil servants, remained loyal or chose silent neutrality, and the regime adapted to shrinking resources and sanctions by redirecting its expenses.

This resilience can be attributed to: a wide support base; effective strategies of ideological, political and sectarian mobilisation; tested coup-proofing and regime security methods; a capacity for military adaptation; and the complex calculations of key social groups and individuals about their interests and alignments. It also stemmed from the ruling clique's conviction that the struggle was of an existential nature; that making meaningful concessions would project weakness, thus inviting more pressure and splitting regime ranks; and that there were acceptable outcomes short of a complete recovery to pre-March 2011 conditions.

Strategies of mobilisation

For the Syrian regime, staving off the political challenge to Assad rule necessitated tailored responses. Indeed, the various segments of the population supporting it differed in their motivations, and in their levels of mobilisation and commitment. To each of these constituencies, the regime devised specific messages, with varying degrees of success. In some cases, it was enough for the regime to secure a group's neutrality or passivity; in other cases, the target group had to be mobilised.

A narrative was crafted to appeal to these audiences: a conspiracy backed by the West, Israel, the Gulf states and Turkey and implemented by Islamist and criminal gangs was assaulting the Syrian state and champion of Arabism for its regional alliances, political steadfastness and secular character. In the regime's rhetoric, this array of forces was portrayed as extremely powerful and yet vulnerable to defeat by societal mobilisation and fortitude. State television and the private *Dunia* channel, owned by a relative of Maher al-Assad, played a key role in disseminating these narratives. They ran shows purporting to expose the dark forces behind the rebellion and praising the security forces and the military, with Assad invariably portrayed as a providential saviour. Pro-regime media highlighted visits by foreign delegations sympathetic to the regime, and the Syrian Electronic Army (a hacking group) waged war online to counter the revolutionary narrative. In private, Assad and his aides held meetings with public figures, including religious leaders, businessmen and judges, to ensure their loyalty through persuasion or threats. The regime also derived some legitimacy from the continued support of senior Sunni religious figures, such as

Mufti Ahmad Hassoun and the prominent preacher Sheikh Said Ramadan al-Butti.

Public displays of loyalty and regime-backed demonstrations ensued, bringing together hardcore supporters (the self-named *menhebakjiyyeh*, or 'those who love you [Assad]') but also large numbers of Syrians working for the government, state-controlled companies or private enterprises in the cities. To all these audiences, Assad presented himself as the last line of defence against contagious state collapse and the repetition of tragedies in the neighbouring countries, a message that resonated at home and abroad. 'Syria is the hub now in this region. It is the fault line, and if you play with the ground you will cause an earthquake,' he told a Western newspaper. 'Do you want to see another Afghanistan, or tens of Afghanistans? ... Any problem in Syria will burn the whole region. If the plan is to divide Syria, that is to divide the whole region.'[11]

As the fighting spread and engulfed urban centres, Assad was forced to adapt his narrative. While at first blaming the violence on Islamist and criminal gangs and presenting his response as law enforcement and counter-terrorism, he finally acknowledged in June 2012 that Syria was in a 'state of war'. The language of total war was employed and aimed to rally crucial segments of society into total mobilisation. Instances of violence against minority members, whether true or fabricated, were amplified in regime media. Local communal self-defence groups, recruited mostly from minorities, obtained greater resources and responsibilities to police their areas. The National Defence Force (allegedly designed after and trained by Iranian Bassiji and Pasdaran units) served as an umbrella for disparate, unevenly organised paramilitary units. Shia fighters, including Lebanese and Iraqis, were deployed around the holy site of Sayyida Zeinab, southeast of Damascus. Armed Christians patrolled their neighbourhoods in Aleppo, Damascus, Maaloula and Homs. Alawite women were recruited into defence units in the city of Homs,[12] and a separate, Alawite-dominated militia known as the *shabbiha* served as an offensive force, deployed to fight alongside the military but also to spread terror.

The most important such audience for this new message of total war was the Alawite community. The crude strategy has been to equate their fate with the regime's survival and to exploit its deep-seated fears about loss of standing and retribution. The organic, if manipulated, link between regime and sect was exacerbated by a widely shared expectation that a Sunni victory would translate into sectarian cleansing. Car bombings, including a massive explosion in the Alawite district of Mezze 86 in Damascus in November 2012, seemed to justify the fear of an impending jihadi slaughter of Alawite heretics.[13]

A sense of siege rekindled the community's survival instincts. Many felt that the regime's strategy had not been brutal enough: Assad's assumed moderation was unfavourably compared with the ruthlessness of his brother Maher, the commander of the elite Republican Guard and 4th Division.[14] Alawite officers and non-commissioned officers were expected to maintain cohesion and loyalty in the ranks. Alawite-dominated elite units were deployed in the most crucial areas in Damascus and the coastal region but also to defend and retake key cities such as Homs and Aleppo. The growing death toll among Alawite fighters and the resulting funerals served to solidify loyalty to the regime and coalesce the sect's support around the military.

Of course, the regime's strategy was not without flaws. Alawite families sought refuge in their home villages, abandoning important cities where their presence contributed to government control. The atmosphere of fear, the mounting loss of life, and the escalating demands on individuals and communities stirred some debate over a repressive strategy that put the whole community at risk and so exacerbated intra-Alawite tensions. The sect had unevenly benefitted from 42 years of Assad rule and many of its members held grudges against the regime. In September

2012, relatives and critics of Assad clashed in his hometown of Qordaha.[15] These instances of discord were, however, effectively contained internally: overall, dissent was seen as coming at the cost of the community's general safety and, two years into the uprising, no major clan had parted ways with the regime.

For domestic audiences that had a political, rather than an organic, attachment to the regime, Assad's emphasis was on the presumed radical nature of the opposition and the threat to the state and its character. Indeed, many Syrians supported the Assad regime out of belief that it embodied the state, promoted religious moderation and prevented chaos. This message also appealed to the multi-confessional urban middle class and the large number of bureaucrats and public sector employees whose status and benefits depended on the regime. To keep this large constituency on side, Assad had to maintain the illusion of a state that continued to function properly under his authority. The holding of elections and the largely uninterrupted payment of salaries to state employees served that purpose.

The complex motivations of significant groups of fence-sitters also slowed the regime's political erosion. Political cynicism about the democratic potential of Syrian society ran deep among minorities and urbanites, many of whom shared the view that the regime had offered reasonable concessions to an uncompromising opposition.[16] The perception that the revolutionaries, with their presumed Islamist, conservative and peasant background, opposed modernity and would question the tenets of economic liberalisation compounded these fears. This was especially the case with the cosmopolitan business elites of Damascus and Aleppo, which had become a mainstay of Assad rule and had considerably more to lose than the poor working classes of the periphery.

However, a rising death toll and the spread of violence to cities threatened the fundamental bargain struck by the regime with the middle and upper classes and the minorities: it no longer provided security and prosperity in exchange for loyalty and political disengagement. Western and Arab sanctions affected the middle and upper classes' financial interests, while fighting, restrictions and shrinking demand slowed the operations of their factories and businesses. The merchant elite, which was required early in the unrest to contribute funding and demonstrate public support, showed signs of hedging and dissent as the challenge to Assad amplified. Even then, the regime expected that rebel abuses, overreach and fragmentation would cost the revolution potential sympathisers and prevent fence-sitters from shifting their loyalty. In short, it calculated that the hardships of war would drive many into a state of political apathy instead of engagement.

The regime also struck local quid pro quos with fence-sitting groups. It agreed to local accommodation in the governorate of Suweida with Druze chieftains eager to prevent their territory from becoming a battlefield between government forces and Sunni rebels.[17] Calculating that the main Kurdish factions could be lured into not embracing the rebellion, the government offered long-awaited citizenship to 300,000 Kurds.[18] It later withdrew its troops from the Kurdish area in the northeast, freeing up forces and creating a thorn in the side of the opposition, which struggled to strike a political agreement with the KNC.

Assad benefitted from the quasi-neutrality of many members of minority groups and the support of key religious and business figures – Christians in particular, as discussed above. Mistrust among many minority communities of the promises of pluralism offered by the Syrian opposition played into the regime's hands – the fear was that these promises would be undercut by armed groups' actual power. The elections of Abdel Baset Sida, a Kurd, and later of George Sabra, a Christian, as successive heads of the Syrian National Council were met with derision among minority members who suspected Islamist forces inside the opposition of hiding behind such figureheads.

The political response

Just as Assad denounced a foreign conspiracy and treacherous domestic elements to mobilise certain sections of the population, he also offered political concessions and a national dialogue. These were primarily designed to split the domestic opposition by catering to the so-called 'loyal opposition' (small leftist and nationalist parties that do not challenge the authority of Assad). They also aimed to create the semblance of progress to nervous domestic audiences that yearned for a political opening, however limited, and to signal to regional audiences that the government showed greater responsiveness to domestic grievances than in other Arab states. Such motions were essential to bolster the claims of Assad's allies, notably Russia, Iran and Hizbullah, that there was a genuine domestic process of reform in place, but that it was being derailed by foreign intervention.

These measures were announced in public speeches and entailed the formation of new governments in April 2011 and June 2012,[19] the release of some political prisoners, and the lifting of the 48-year-old emergency law. The regime also launched a National Dialogue that put forward constitutional amendments, approved by referendum in February 2012, that included: the removal of Article 8 from the constitution that referred to the Ba'ath Party as the 'leading party in the society and the state'; the creation of a new political party law; permission for more than one candidate to run in the presidential election; term limits on the presidential mandate; and economic and social reforms. According to the regime, the turnout was 57.4%, and the approval rate was 89.4%.[20] National elections for a new parliament followed in May, and official turnout was 51%.[21] The inclusion of the 'loyal opposition' did not prevent Ba'athist and regime-aligned candidates posing as independents from winning an overwhelming victory. In both polls, the absence of independent monitors cast considerable doubt on official figures while reporting suggested a much lower turnout.[22]

These elections were primarily designed to maintain the semblance of a functioning state and stem Assad's loss of legitimacy by staging public displays of support. However, the regime's reformist theatrics and co-optation of minor opposition figures failed to mollify the protest movement. By then, it had become clear that power no longer resided in the formal institutions of the state but in top regime circles and the security services.

Adapting military strategy

The disproportionality of the regime's military response demonstrated both a mindset that placed security above compromise and an early desire to alter the nature of the uprising so as to provoke an armed conflict that could be met with its extensive coercive apparatus. Once it became clear that the rebellion was too strong to be entirely quashed, the regime adjusted its approach in the expectation that the societal and humanitarian cost of the war and the rebels' own abuses and mistakes in governing liberated areas would eventually alienate the civilian population. Competition over ideology, territory, tactics and resources as well as the trials of fighting a war would later fragment the rebel front.

The government's initial strategy was to deploy overwhelming force to crush protests and rebels, while undertaking quiet outreach to local chieftains. It combined traditional security operations in most cities (monitoring and arrest of activists, intimidation, torture, plus some accommodation of the local population) with a deployment of military assets in rural areas where the challenge was greater. As the armed resistance expanded, the regime utilised the full-spectrum of its conventional firepower: it deployed infantry and armoured capabilities starting in the spring of 2011, artillery in the autumn of 2011, air power in the spring of 2012, cluster bombs in the summer of 2012, and missiles (including *Scuds*) in the autumn of 2012.

This strategy of gradual escalation had the dual effect of testing, then crossing, presumed international norms and red lines and of desensitising audiences, at home and abroad, to the human toll. It also laid the groundwork for the potential use of chemical weapons, albeit in small-scale and deniable ways. It is notable that the regime did not adopt a counter-insurgency strategy aimed at securing and regaining the loyalty of the population. Its 220,000-strong army was trained for conventional warfare against Israel and its 50,000-strong elite units to put down internal challenges brutally.[23]

The regime forces demonstrated varying levels of competence and fighting skills. The regular military, comprising units of differing quality and loyalty, proved incapable of conducting joint armoured-infantry operations or coordinating ground-air operations. It focused on securing static assets and supply routes, but was undermined from within by loss of life, desertions and low morale. Concerns about defections made the infantry less deployable, forcing the recourse to air power and artillery and causing immense human and material damage. The regime's armoured capabilities were threatened by anti-tank weaponry seized from bases, and its air dominance was challenged by the rebels' capture of military airports and possession of anti-aircraft artillery. In many cases, civilian combatants possessed better situational knowledge and intelligence than Assad forces. Elite units however fared better: by late 2012, they had recovered ground in Homs, checked the rebel campaign in Aleppo and cleared much of the immediate vicinity of Damascus.

In the absence of internationally enforced no-fly zones, air power offered the regime a qualitative edge over the rebels and the option of not deploying a tired and unreliable infantry. Helicopters ferried supplies and undertook reconnaissance, while attack helicopters targeted civilian areas as well as rebel units. As importantly, air power served to terrorise the population and create rifts between rebels and civilians, as the latter attributed bombardments to the former's presence.

Facing an adapting and widening insurgency that benefitted from local support and better knowledge of the terrain, from mid-2012 the regime was forced to adapt its strategy around its shrinking capabilities and reach. It defined certain areas as essential for survival: Damascus, Aleppo, the central region (including the cities of Homs and Hama), the highways linking them and the infrastructure supporting them. It particularly sought to secure the outer ring of Jabal al-Nusayriyah. The military proved able to score tactical victories in urban settings thanks to massive shelling and the blockade of rebel-friendly areas. Over time, government forces chose to ignore areas deemed as unimportant or irretrievable, often resorting to artillery and air-strikes to pummel them. A key objective for the regime was to prevent the gathering and organisation of large rebel units on Syrian soil, a task for which air power was used.

A key factor in the survival of the regime was the sidelining of institutions. The inconsequential impact on the regime of the defection of Prime Minister Riyad Hijab in August 2012 illustrates this new reality, and the extent to which the instruments of government had been hollowed out. Even the Ba'ath Party was marginalised: unable to ensure the proper functioning of local administrations, its dense national and local networks were diverted for the purpose of repression. Its hated status in society made it a convenient sacrificial lamb when the new constitution abolished its role as 'the leader of the state and society'. The loyal central command was gutted of any meaningful political purpose, which helps to explain the strong fall in voter turnout in 2012 compared with previous elections. Meanwhile, many of its disgruntled members in rural areas joined the uprising.

Early on, the regime underwrote the transformation of criminal gangs called the *shabbiha* into paramilitary units. Directly controlled by Assad's relatives and financed by regime associates, the shadowy *shabbiha* were particularly useful in providing a degree of deniability that could confuse foreign observers and media. Though not exclusively Alawites, they played a leading role in imposing terror in Sunni villages at the periphery of the Alawite region and in assisting the military in clearing out urban areas. They were responsible for a series of atrocities committed against civilians, including massacres in villages such as Houla, the first on such a large scale, in May 2012.

Early expectations that the military would either fragment or mount a coup were frustrated. The unclear fate of Defence Minister General Ali Habib in the early days of the uprising – though rumours of his death circulated, he was sidelined for allegedly opposing a harsh crackdown – suggested to some that the Syrian army might remove Assad in the way the military in Tunisia and Egypt helped oust their presidents. However this did not come to bear and the assassinations in July 2012 of senior generals, including Assad's brother-in-law and Head of Intelligence Assef Shawkat and Defence Minister Dawoud Rajha, failed to disrupt military operations meaningfully. The defection of General Manaf Tlass, scion of a key Sunni military family associated with the regime, also had minimal impact. Defections and desertions certainly affected performance, cohesion and morale, and cumulatively could debilitate the regular military. Yet, crucially, no large unit in its entirety had shifted loyalty by early 2013. The top operational command also proved dependable: despite up to 100 army brigadiers and generals defecting or deserting, the impact has been minimal as the Syrian military is top-heavy and many of these officers were retired or marginal players.

The loyalty of the military is largely due to the philosophy that underpinned the organisation of the security sector: regime survival superseded military efficiency. The security sector was built not only to guard the regime against potential external and domestic threats, but also to do so without posing a threat to the regime. The multiplication of security agencies, its politicised human capital and a preferential allocation of resources to units deemed more loyal (to build devoted, albeit competing, security agencies) was meant to protect the regime without creating challenges from within. As a result, defections largely occurred in regular units rather than elite troops, ironically leaving the regime with a more loyal and deployable core.

The limits of resilience

Despite surviving for longer than many expected (Western and Arab officials as well as many Syrian oppositionists have measured Assad's remaining time in weeks or months throughout the conflict), it seems unlikely that his strategies can decisively stop, let alone reverse, the erosion of his legitimacy, resources, territorial reach, and military power – or even allow these to persist in a diminished and retrenched manner. Assad himself has promised swift victory several times, only to see the rebellion gain steam. While still large, his support base can only contract. His best hopes are that Syrians will not join revolutionary ranks and that the opposition will decisively fragment over resources, ideology and political competition before dislodging him. Having alienated many of his neighbours, Assad can expect continuous challenges from abroad, while the security vacuum in Syria can only suck regional powers into the conflict.

Moreover, all of the regime's sources of power continue to be strangled. The army is losing considerable manpower, with 20 or 30 soldiers killed daily and peaks of 50 fatalities during major operations.[24] Three to four times that number have been injured and can no longer fight. While the regime can tap into minorities and regime sympathisers to form local defence groups, civilian fighters are of a lower quality than normal soldiers. The cumulative effect of defections and desertions has undoubtedly taken a toll on the military's performance and morale.

Its hardware has also suffered: though not yet incapacitating, the loss of helicopters, aircraft and armoured vehicles point to the erosion of his qualitative edge as rebels obtain better weapons. As a result, the regime's dependence on external military help has increased. While the local defence industry remains able to produce small and light weaponry and ammunition, maintaining his military superiority requires Iranian and Russian assistance.

The regime's resources have also been battered and it has few sources of revenue left to be able to sustain the fight indefinitely. Its foreign reserves have shrunk from US$18bn before the revolution[25] to an estimated US$3–5bn by late 2012.[26] The collapse of the economy has considerably reduced its tax base and it is losing hard currency due to US and EU sanctions on energy exports and as rebel groups capture oil fields in the northeast. Iran has helped Syria circumvent Western sanctions and provided credit lines, but Syria's sole financial underwriter has competing priorities to balance with its support for Assad and limited resources as well. Assets of regime associates have been frozen, and there are reports that major Syrian businessmen have transferred or sheltered their wealth abroad.[27] As privations increase, the regime must provide food, gas, medicines and gasoline to Assad's various constituencies to ensure their loyalty.

The result is that state spending has decreased in many areas.[28] The regime does not seek to regain the loyalty of the entire population through state largesse or vast spending on reconstruction, and has ceased to fund education, health and other services in areas it has lost or considers hostile. The shift to a war economy, whereby people pay, often at a premium, for services and goods that were once provided or subsidised, similarly reduces the strain on Assad's finances. A major source of income for the government are two mobile phone operators, MTN and the Makhlouf-owned Syriatel, whose revenues have soared.[29] Some regime figures have contributed to funding the repression, especially the *shabbiha* and local defence committees, and state employees have been asked to contribute part of their salaries to state coffers to finance the war effort, as have businessmen and other professionals. The collapse of the Syrian currency, which fluctuated wildly before stabilising at around 70 Syrian pounds to the dollar, marginally benefits the state's financial situation. The deteriorating situation put a halt on internal consumption of high-end imported goods but also fired inflation, which improved the state's balance sheet. Ironically, the influx of cash from Syrian expatriates and foreign funders to sustain their relatives and the rebellion also contributed to mitigating the economic consequences and the pressure on the Syrian pound.

After two years of conflict, the Assad regime remains the dominant fighting force in Syria and still enjoys significant backing, both domestically and from abroad. To its constituency, its narrative has been vindicated by the radicalisation of the opposition and the descent of the country into civil war. But the shrinking of the Assad regime, politically, militarily and territorially, is likely irreversible. As it contracts, however, the bigger question is whether it can survive in a diminished manner or whether it too will fragment should Assad lose control over the capital Damascus.

Notes

1   Balanche, *La region alaouite et le pouvoir syrien*.

2   The casualty figures for Hama remain disputed and range between 10 and 40,000.

3   'Governor Iyad Ghazal outlines his "Dream of Homs"', *Wikileaks*.

4   Balanche, 'Geographie de la revolte syrienne', *Outre-Terre*, Octobre–Decembre 2011, pp.437–458.

5   Rania Abouzeid, 'Who Will the Tribes Back in Syria's Civil War?', *Time*, 10 October 2012, http://world. time.com/2012/10/10/who-will-the-tribes-back-in-syrias-civil-war/.

6   Interviews with several tribal leaders from the Deir Ez-Zor and Raqqah provinces, Doha and Antakya, September 2011 and April 2012.

7   Interviews with Kurdish activists from the KNC and SNC, Istanbul, April 2012, and Beirut, November 2012.

8   Marlin Dick, 'Swaida: resistance in quiet part of Syria', *The Daily*

Star, 8 January 2013, http://www.dailystar.com.lb/News/Middle-East/2013/Jan-08/201228-swaida-resistance-in-quiet-part-of-syria.ashx#axzz2IS2lpUX1.

9   See: 'Muthahirat madinat al-salmiyya', YouTube, 1 April 2011, https://www.youtube.com/watch?v=JoidN8Didxo; 'Tathahirat madinat al-salmiyya – Hama juma'at "lan nirka'a"', YouTube, 12 August 2011, https://www.youtube.com/watch?v=uZoeG98c0-8; and 'Bidayat al-tashbi' al-shahid jamal ali al-fakhuri', YouTube, 30 June 2012, https://www.youtube.com/watch?v=gK4kjNsyUrM.

10 A popular theory among some Levantine intellectual and political circles holds that minorities (Christians, Shia, Alawites and Druze) need to unify politically to fend off the Sunni majority, pejoratively and simplistically referred to as a 'Sea of Sunnis'. See: Emile Hokayem, 'A simplistic sectarian lens magnifies extremist agenda', *The National*, 30 July 2012, http://www.thenational.ae/thenationalconversation/comment/a-simplistic-sectarian-lens-magnifies-extremist-agenda.

11 Andrew Gilligan, 'Assad: challenge Syria at your peril', *The Telegraph*, 29 October 2011, http://www.telegraph.co.uk/news/worldnews/middleeast/syria/8857898/Assad-challenge-Syria-at-your-peril.html.

12 Loveday Morris, 'Assad's Lionesses: the female last line in the battle for Syria', *The Independent*, 22 January 2013, http://www.independent.co.uk/news/world/middle-east/assads-lionesses-the-female-last-line-in-the-battle-for-syria-8462221.html.

13 Khaled Yacoub Oweis and Mohammed Abbas, 'Syrian rebels fire at, miss Assad's palace', Reuters, 7 November 2012, http://in.reuters.com/article/2012/11/07/syria-damascus-bombs-idINDEE8A603020121107.

14 Interviews with Christian and Alawite businessmen, Beirut, November 2011 and June 2012.

15 'Chroniques du délitement. 2 / Règlement de comptes à Qardaha, antre de la famille Al Assad', *Le Monde*, 1 October 2012, http://syrie.blog.lemonde.fr/2012/10/01/chroniques-du-delitement-2-reglement-de-comptes-a-qardaha-antre-de-la-famille-al-assad/.

16 Interviews with Sunni, Christian and Alawite middle- and upper-class professionals, Beirut, May and November 2011, and Dubai, May and November 2012.

17 Interviews with Syrian and Lebanese Druze, Beirut, January and July 2012.

18 'Syrian president grants citizenship to Kurds', *The Telegraph*, 7 April 2011, http://www.telegraph.co.uk/news/worldnews/middleeast/syria/8435041/Syrian-president-grants-citizenship-to-Kurds.html.

19 Prime Minister Riyad Hijab, appointed in June 2012, defected in August and was quickly replaced. 'Syrian Prime Minister Riad Hijab defects', *BBC News*, 6 August 2012, http://www.bbc.co.uk/news/world-middle-east-19146380.

20 'Syria says voters approve new constitution', *Ahram Online*, 27 February 2012, http://english.ahram.org.eg/NewsContent/2/8/35548/World/Region/Syria-says-voters-approve-new-constitution.aspx.

21 'Syria Says Voter Turnout 51 Percent in Boycotted Election', *Voice of*

America, 15 May 2012, http://www.voanews.com/content/syria_voter_turnout_election/666503.html.

22 Neil MacFarquhar 'Syrians Vote in Election Dismissed by Foes as a Farce', *The New York Times*, 7 May 2012, http://www.nytimes.com/2012/05/08/world/middleeast/syrians-vote-in-parliamentary-elections.html?pagewanted=all&_r=0.

23 *The Military Balance 2013*, (Abingdon: Routledge for the IISS, 2013).

24 'Syria: Foreign intervention still debated, but distant', IISS *Strategic Comments*, vol. 18, no. 28, September 2012, http://www.iiss.org/publications/strategic-comments/past-issues/volume-18-2012/september/syria-foreign-intervention-still-debated-but-distant/.

25 Suleiman Al-Khalidi, 'Syria's war-battered pound floats on rebel funds', Reuters, 23 December 2012, http://www.reuters.com/article/2012/12/23/us-syria-crisis-currency-idUSBRE8BM05920121223.

26 Interviews with: European officials London, July 2012; and Paris, October 2012; and Arab officials, Manama, December 2012.

27 Interviews with Syrian businessmen, Beirut, November 2011 and July 2012, and Dubai, May 2012.

28 Michael Peel, 'Syria central banker rebuts crisis claims', *Financial Times*, 4 October 2012, http://www.ft.com/intl/cms/s/0/348f2c14-0cb1-11e2-a73c-00144feabdc0.html#axzz2LAV1d8Mm.

29 Peel, 'Syria finds means of financial survival', *Financial Times*, 12 February 2013, http://www.ft.com/cms/s/0/1bc9ad28-6a1f-11e2-a7d2-00144feab49a.html#axzz2RPWYbAhb.

CHAPTER THREE

The rise of the opposition

Prior to the uprising, Syria's traditional opposition appeared fragmented and dejected. It comprised ageing Islamist, liberal, leftist and nationalist figures and factions that had struggled to maintain a public profile, coalesce and mount a significant challenge to the Assad regime. While several opposition groups operated in exile, notably the Muslim Brotherhood (MB), many oppositionists remained in Syria. Outmanoeuvred by Assad and disconnected from the grievances and outlook of Syria's youth, it was particularly ill-equipped to foment and lead an uprising.

The emergence of many oppositions

The decade prior to the uprising did witness moments of mobilisation. The Damascus Spring of 2000–2001, which was ultimately squashed by the regime, allowed for public meetings of dissidents and intellectuals who elaborated programmes and advocated political reforms. The perceived weakening of the Assad regime in 2005 encouraged a broad section of Syrian dissidents to call for gradual and peaceful democratic liberalisation and the normalisation of relations with Lebanon in the Beirut-Damascus Declaration.[1] The regime successfully resisted these efforts and, as they came on the heels of international pressure, portrayed them as treasonous and jailed their advocates.[2]

The traditional opposition at home found it difficult to organise and inspire, despite the fact that it included respected individuals representing a broad but ageing section of Syrian society, from businessman turned independent parliamentarian Riaf Seif and Alawite economist Aref Dallila, to Christian oppositionist Michel Kilo and Islamist-leaning judge Haitham al-Maleh. Low-level dissent also extended to urban merchant families that had not been co-opted by the state and to a new class of intellectuals and artists. These dissidents, who often lacked deep connections to Syria's fast-changing but still largely apolitical society, overwhelmingly advocated gradual reform rather than brutal regime change.

Meanwhile, the opposition abroad demonstrated political ineptitude: in 2006, the MB and political exiles formed the National Salvation Front with the recently defected but despised Vice-President Abdel-Halim Khaddam. This unlikely coalition, founded just as Assad came under international pressure for his role in Lebanon, failed to resonate inside Syria and was tainted by suspicions that it was a proxy of the US and Saudi Arabia.

The networks of activists

In parallel to the traditional opposition, an apolitical civil society was growing, though at a slow pace. Ironically, an effort to strengthen civil society had been spearheaded by the regime in order to project an image of progress, mobilise urban youth and offset the state's diminishing capability. Asma al-Assad, the president's wife, played a key role by establishing and encouraging the formation of state-backed non-governmental organisations in the fields of health, education, culture and social work. Alongside these well-funded and well-publicised organisations, grassroots groups formed to cope with the consequences of the decay of the state, growing poverty and unemployment and the influx of rural migrants into suburban areas. Many activists were engaged in social-welfare activities, including the provision of basic services to the population. Religious networks and charities were also allowed to operate in this social sphere.

These loose organisations, which operated on the margins of the state and without official authorisation, in many cases, provided the militant core that led the initial protests. Motivated by the same set of economic, social and political grievances and demands that drove other Arab uprisings, youth activists in and around major cities were responsible for bringing ideological and organisational coherence to what began as a disparate protest movement. By April 2011, they had set up Local Coordination Committees (LCCs) across the country, which coordinated nationwide peaceful protests every Friday and ensured that slogans were consistent and forward-looking. Through social media and other forms of communication, activists agreed on the message to be broadcast every week. They also adopted the pre-Ba'ath flag as a symbol of the revolution. As the movement grew, similar grassroots groups emerged, including the Syrian Revolution General Commission and the Higher Council of the Syrian Revolution. The movement widened to include middle-class professionals, as well as urban and rural workers. In cities like Hama and Homs where sympathy for the opposition was strong, protests occurred in central squares; elsewhere, demonstrators mobilised in mosques and local neighbourhoods, as at the Omari Mosque in Deraa and the Umayyad Mosque in Damascus.[3]

Realising the LCCs' potency, the security forces focused on identifying and dismantling these small cells early on, with relative success. However, their leaderless and decentralised character made total eradication impossible. Nevertheless, by depriving the revolution of some of its most forward-looking and idealistic elements, this harsh crackdown contributed to the shift within the protest movement towards more radical forms of opposition. From early 2012, the militarisation of the revolution further divided and marginalised activists, whose means and organisation paled in comparison to those of the rebels.

The dysfunctional dynamics of the political opposition

Just as demonstrations gathered steam, the lack of a recognisable political front to express and promote the demands of the protest movement became a liability. Taken by surprise by the magnitude and peaceful nature of the mobilisation and by the emergence of new demands and new figures, the traditional opposition scrambled to respond.

The precedent of Libya had set high expectations for what the Syrian opposition should look like and could deliver. One should, however, view the Libyan case as a historical aberration. There, opposition figures, based out of a major city that had quickly freed itself from Gadhafi's grip, coalesced quickly to form the National Transitional Council, which was fully empowered to obtain international recognition as Libya's legitimate government and negotiate abroad. High-level defections, which included top intelligence, security and diplomatic officials, occurred within the first weeks of the uprising. Gadhafi's direct and unambiguous threats against civilians and major cities helped unify the opposition. The resort to foreign intervention was uncontested among oppositionists, and the speed with which events occurred in Libya did not allow for the emergence of major divergences. Crucially, Libya's religious and ethnic homogeneity meant that, unlike Syria, massive communal violence was not a major concern and its neighbours remained largely uninvolved.

In comparison, Syria's opposition, while more active than its Libyan counterpart prior to the uprising, emerged as more complex and less organised, reflecting the country's greater diversity and pre-existing divisions. Moreover, it quickly became clear that many of the established opposition figures, at home and abroad, were disconnected from the new grassroots activists, who spearheaded the demonstrations, and later from the armed rebel groups.

Western governments, Gulf states and Turkey launched separate, sometimes conflicting, efforts to groom a Syrian opposition. After years of mostly ignoring Syrian activists, the US and EU struggled to identify and help organise the opposition at home and abroad. The Western reasoning was that a unified and empowered Syrian opposition would serve the dual purpose of representing the wider Syrian popular movement and legitimising diplomacy. The quest for an inclusive and authoritative opposition quickly proved frustrating, and efforts to identify key players inside Syria were made difficult by the ever-changing, organic and organisationally fragmented nature of the uprising. Inside Syria, aside from the co-opted 'loyal opposition' (notably the Syrian Social National Party of Ali Haidar and the People's Will Party of Qadri Jamil), the National Coordination Committee (NCC), an umbrella group of leftist, nationalist and Kurdish factions founded in June 2011, argued for peaceful opposition to the regime.

Abroad, new faces claiming to represent the new opposition organised meetings in Turkey and Qatar. The formation of the Syrian National Council (SNC) was the culmination of this process over the summer of 2011. The SNC, which demanded the unconditional resignation or ouster of Assad, brought together independent opposition figures from liberal, leftist and nationalist backgrounds, as well as unaffiliated Islamists and the MB. It quickly secured Turkish, Qatari and, to a lesser extent, Saudi political and material support. While it did attract some minority members, it lacked meaningful Kurdish, Alawite, Druze or Christian representation. Some opposition figures, including Michel Kilo, chose to remain outside this umbrella organisation, calling it foreign-inspired and manipulated.

It had quickly become clear that Syrian oppositionists were divided over important issues: the militarisation of the uprising; the internationalisation of the crisis; the recourse to foreign intervention; and the merits and modalities of dialogue with the regime. Competition among the opposition groups for internal legitimacy and foreign patronage were at times counter-productive, even petty.

Expectations of the SNC were particularly high, and the challenges it faced were immense. The fledgling, largely powerless and under-resourced organisation (in 2012 it had revenues of US$40m, most of which went to humanitarian relief) struggled to impose political authority over myriad opposition factions. It had to reconcile Islamist and secular forces, federal and unitary tendencies, ethnic and sectarian grievances, as well as generational gaps. Imposing its authority over and channelling funding to armed groups that valued their newfound autonomy (and had developed their own backers) was another key challenge, as was addressing the humanitarian crisis and providing resources to liberated areas, without having adequate funds, access or expertise. It also had to devise an inclusive and comprehensive political platform that could not be hijacked by any one faction, and that would offer meaningful guarantees to Syria's minorities, incentives to fence-sitters and assurances to would-be defectors.

A fundamental problem for the SNC hinged on its position as a body operating from abroad and courting foreign support, while seeking to overcome the perception of being a proxy for outside powers as it sought to appeal to (largely unknown) audiences at home. An early test was its ability to internationalise the crisis and obtain a UN Security Council (UNSC) resolution against Assad. As the UN process floundered over Russian and Chinese objections, the SNC became the primary interlocutor of countries demanding Assad's resignation as part of the 'Friends of Syria' process. Yet, major countries held off granting it full recognition as 'the legitimate representative of the Syrian people' before it demonstrated credibility and competence. A lack of political influence at home – the support of the armed rebels or any domestic mandate to negotiate with Assad – undermined support from its diverse foreign backers and so hampered efforts to engage in internationally endorsed diplomacy towards a transition.

Quickly, it became clear that the bar set for the SNC was too high. It suffered from serious internal dysfunctions as well as factional and personal competition between its members. Its first president, the secular intellectual Burhan Ghalioun, lacked charisma and managerial experience, as did his successors the Kurdish academic Abdul Baset Sida and the Christian Marxist George Sabra. Ghalioun stayed on longer than stipulated in the SNC's charter – a bad omen for an organisation ostensibly dedicated to bringing democracy to Syria.

It also failed to frame the struggle in a way that would offer an inclusive vision to Syria's many hesitant constituencies. Reactive and at times incoherent, its communication strategy reinforced the prejudices held by many Syrians towards the opposition in exile. Instead of serving as a unifying and proactive force, the SNC became defined by its internal struggles and compromises. Many Syrians saw the group's leadership as distant, petty and inefficient. This complicated its messaging toward minorities and fence-sitters, who derived little confidence from seeing its divisive politics at play. The SNC adopted a rigid stance on Syria's Arab identity, thwarting any rapprochement with the moderate Kurdish National Council (KNC). Its increasingly Islamist orientation scared away minority members, especially Christians and Alawites who needed tangible guarantees about a pluralistic post-Assad order, and warily watched Islamists seize power in post-revolutionary Egypt, Libya and Tunisia.

For the SNC, attracting funds to finance rebel operations and humanitarian relief was vital to building credibility and authority inside Syria. The sums raised were however incommensurate with needs and expectations. Many individual contributors preferred to bypass the council and fund specific groups inside Syria. Scarce foreign government funding was no less problematic: Western governments were reluctant to provide funding for lethal assistance, directing their money toward humanitarian relief and support for activists, while the Gulf states displayed blatant political partiality by funding specific groups directly.

Unsurprisingly, the relationship between the SNC and the nominal rebel command structure of the Free Syrian Army (FSA) – two weak organisations plagued with internal splits – proved fraught. The SNC struggled to raise funds and the FSA to unify and coordinate the multiple units of defectors and civilian combatants. Deficient logistics and a scarcity of weaponry and ammunition at important junctures were blamed on both SNC dithering and FSA incompetence.

The SNC was expected to be the face of the Syrian opposition in the international arena. This depended on the ability of its leadership to devise an internal consensus on the strategies of diplomacy, militarisation and intervention – all of which required the sort of leadership and leverage the SNC direly lacked. For many SNC members, diplomacy was primarily a way to expose Assad's duplicity and to force their international allies into more coercive approaches. They distrusted UN-led diplomatic initiatives over concerns that Assad would outmanoeuvre their negotiators and be given a role in any transition. More importantly, the SNC had not garnered enough credibility to muster sufficient domestic support in favour of diplomacy: rebel groups and oppositionists feared it would buy Assad time to recover lost ground and consolidate his position.

The SNC also vacillated on the matter of foreign intervention. While it opposed direct military intervention, it embraced calls for a no-fly zone in December 2011, knowing that there was not yet an international appetite for it. While publicly supporting the militarisation of the uprising as morally right and as a fait accompli, SNC members feared that it would cause the rise of autonomous warlords less likely to defer to political authority, including their own.

A fundamental problem that arose was the supremacy and role of the MB and its allies in internal committees. They formed the majority of the 350-strong SNC, monopolised positions that handled finances and humanitarian relief, and also enjoyed preferential access to the Qatari and Turkish governments, as well as better media access through *al-Jazeera*. Anger over the MB's domination of SNC policy and favouritism towards its own militias inside Syria drove prominent secular and independent members away. Among those who left or froze their membership in the SNC were Basma Kodmani, a prominent liberal intellectual; Rima Fleihan, a senior Druze activist; Kamal Labwani, a veteran secular dissident; and Haitham al-Maleh, an Islamist-leaning former judge.

The SNC disappoints, the National Coalition steps in

By the middle of 2012, Syrian and international disappointment with the performance of the SNC had peaked. A series of meetings intended to improve the functioning of the umbrella group and coordinate with other factions of the opposition failed to deliver tangible results. There was a sense that international support would fade barring a profound transformation of the Syrian opposition. Furthermore, the Assad government sought to discredit the revolution by emphasising the SNC's internal divisions, ineffectiveness and foreign backing.

In October 2012, Riad Seif, a respected dissident who had played a quiet role in the setting-up of the SNC but remained outside its leadership structure, launched a political effort to create another umbrella coalition. The Syrian National Initiative (SNI) was aimed at broader representation of the various opposition groups, at unifying rebel ranks under its political authority and at forming a transitional government to administer liberated areas and run the country after the fall of the regime.[4] Alienated by the bullying tactics of the MB and worried about the fragmentation of the opposition, many secular politicians supported Seif.

This effort attracted the support of the US and several European countries. In a major rebuke, then US Secretary of State Hillary Clinton dramatically announced that '[the US] made it clear that the SNC can no longer be viewed as the visible leader of the opposition ... The opposition must include people from inside Syria and others who have a legitimate voice that needs to be heard.'[5] The initiative received the quiet backing of Saudi Arabia, Jordan and the UAE. Alarmed by the MB's influence within the SNC, all calculated that a new coalition would dilute its weight and provide for stronger secular representation. A similarly powerful motivation was to form a political front able to resist the rise of radical Islamist groups and devise a pluralistic political platform.

The SNI provided the blueprint for the National Coalition of Syrian Revolutionary and Opposition Forces (NC), which came into being in November 2012. It owed much to Qatari, Emirati and Turkish mediation between the various factions, but also to expectations that the new alliance would receive quick recognition and ultimately greater assistance from Western states. While its membership was tighter, the leadership of the NC represented a broader section of Syrian society. It was headed by Sheikh Moaz al-Khatib, a moderate cleric and engineer, with Riad Seif and Suhair Atassi, a female activist from a prominent family who had joined revolutionary ranks in its early days, as his deputies. All three enjoyed significant credibility for belonging to the internal opposition (and both al-Khatib and Seif had been jailed for their political activism). It associated more closely with local activist networks and the various Military Councils (MCs) being set up across the country. After much hesitation and pressure from Qatar and Turkey, a restructured SNC also joined the NC. Although diluted, the MB's influence in the new organisation remained considerable as senior SNC members and MB-affiliated individuals were granted membership in the NC. Furthermore, the NC failed to convince the main Kurdish coalition to join.

The NC defined three key priorities. Firstly, it sought greater international support, so as to build institutional capacity. Weeks after its formation, it obtained political recognition as the 'sole representative of the Syrian people' from 140 countries at a 'Friends of Syria' meeting in Marrakesh. The next political move was to form a transitional government, to administer liberated areas and plan for a post-Assad context, with the hope that such a government would obtain international legal recognition. Secondly, was a renewed effort to unify rebel ranks under the SMC, established in December 2012. Thirdly, conscious of the failure of the SNC to address the fears of Syria's minorities, al-Khatib embarked on a public campaign to emphasise that any post-Assad order would be pluralistic and would guarantee political, religious and social rights to all citizens.[6]

The viability of the NC's initiatives and the overall credibility of the coalition remained contingent upon adequate funding – al-Khatib estimated that a transitional government would need US$3bn in financing.[7] However, this remained a distant goal: led by the US, several of the NC's foreign allies demanded political consolidation and greater effectiveness on matters of local governance and humanitarian assistance before upping their direct commitment. The US in particular was insistent that the NC include Syrian defectors in its transitional planning in an effort to assuage former Assad loyalists, including former Prime Minister Riyad Hijab and other technocrats. These defectors were, however, viewed with suspicion by many oppositionists – for example, the MB opposed the nomination of Hijab as a transitional prime minister. Other countries, notably France, pressed for the rapid formation of a government in exile, which would open the door for greater financial support and facilitate military options, such as the provision of weaponry.

Syria's Kurds: opportunity or danger?

For Syria's 2m-strong Kurdish community, the unrest offered an opportunity to seek redress for historical injustices, state neglect and political disenfranchisement, most notably the denial of citizenship to as many as 300,000 people. The weakening of a state that proved oppressive, manipulative, and oblivious to their needs presented new political options for them.[8]

However, the uprising itself contains elements that could, absent a political agreement with the opposition, exacerbate Arab-Kurdish and Islamist-Kurdish tensions. The Kurds' political diversity and dispersed geographical distribution along Syria's northern regions have made them vulnerable to entanglement in an array of escalating local dynamics that have come into play since the uprising, exacerbated by their own internal divisions. On a regional level, Turkish and Iraqi interests in Syria, and the potential for Iranian foul play, expose them to the risk of manipulation from outside.

So far, no consensus exists among Kurds as to an ultimate but realistic objective for them within Syria. For many, the model to replicate is that of Iraq's Kurds: an autonomous region within a federal state, enabling them to assert their distinct identity, lay claim to resources and cultivate external alliances. Others harbour a more ambitious vision of full Kurdish independence: a state carved out of Kurdish-populated territories in Syria, Iraq, Turkey and Iran.

The main political fault line in the Kurdish community reflects these conflicting agendas. On the more moderate end of the spectrum is the KNC, which is a coalition of relatively weak parties established in October 2011 with the backing of Massoud Barzani, the powerful leader of Iraq's Kurdish Regional Government (KRG) and the Kurdish Democratic Party (KDP). Barzani's ties to Turkey make him an important ally whom the KNC cannot afford to alienate on account of the strategic depth and political and material support he and, by extension, Turkey provide.

There is also the more radical Democratic Union Party (PYD), the Syrian associate of Turkey's Kurdish separatist movement the Kurdistan Workers' Party (PKK). With its well-organised armed wing, the PYD's ethos and internal functioning mirror those of the PKK. The latter has benefitted from the collapse of the Syrian state as it has been able to use Syrian territory as a haven as it escalated attacks in Turkey throughout 2011 and 2012. The PKK's calculations, and by extension those of the PYD, may change should the ceasefire announced by the PKK's leader Abdullah Ocalan in March 2013 open the way for a settlement of the Kurdish question in Turkey.

Since 2011, rhetoric has escalated as the KNC and the PYD have competed to represent the Kurdish community politically and govern Kurdish-dominated regions. While the PYD deployed its fighters in Kurdish-populated areas and occupied government facilities, the KNC has had less muscle to flex. The PYD presents itself as the community's best protector against Arab and Islamist fighters, in comparison to the more accommodationist KNC. This intra-Kurdish struggle has been temporarily contained thanks to the mediation of Barzani and a Supreme Kurdish Committee, formed to foster internal dialogue, establish security arrangements and present a united front to the non-Kurdish opposition and central government. The détente remains, however, vulnerable to intra-Kurdish dynamics and to external threats.

From the perspective of the Syrian regime, the Kurdish community was seen, early on, as a target for manipulation. It offered citizenship to stateless Kurds after decades of denial – a move that was widely interpreted as a cynical ploy to drive a wedge between them and the non-Kurdish revolutionaries. Assad later withdrew most of his troops from the Kurdish areas, gauging that Kurds would thereafter inevitably clash with Arab rebels, opening a new armed and politicised front sure to bog down the latter. The ensuing security vacuum would also check

Turkey by creating instability on its southern border. By late 2012, the regime's calculations appeared to have been correct.

Indeed, even as Kurdish youth activists showed enthusiasm for the revolution, the main factions largely remained on the sidelines of the conflict. They calculated that, regardless of the outcome, the weakening of the Syrian state would work to their advantage, and that the priority was to shelter their region from the fighting and havoc that engulfed the country. Furthermore, the new Syrian opposition was unknown to them: many of its members espoused an Arab nationalist outlook that disregarded Kurdish cultural and political rights, and an Islamist one at odds with the Kurds' more secular social mores.

Failed negotiations with the SNC throughout 2011 and 2012 heightened long-seated fears about Arab chauvinism as the Kurdish demand for fully-fledged federalism rather than decentralisation was rejected. Ghalioun, then leader of the SNC, provocatively said: 'There is no such thing as Syrian Kurdistan.'[9] The radicalisation of the uprising empowered Islamist fighters with links to Iraq's Sunni community and the Arab Gulf states, two actors deeply distrusted by the Kurds.

Clashes between Kurdish fighters and rebels occurred in several ethnically mixed areas, such as Aleppo and the northeast.[10] The most intense fighting was in January 2013: PYD militiamen fought with FSA and Islamist factions that had entered the ethnically mixed and regime-free town of Ras al-Ayn (Serekaniye in Kurdish). Such incidents, which revived ingrained Kurdish distrust of Arab factions and suspicions of Turkish mischief, strengthened the position of the PYD as the self-declared protector of its community. Another consequence of the conflict was the movement of Kurdish refugees from Damascus, Aleppo, and southern and western parts of the country towards the Kurdish-dominated northeast and into Iraqi Kurdistan. This was welcomed by the Kurdish political leadership: despite the humanitarian suffering, this movement was seen by some as contributing to the constitution of an ethnically more homogenous region.

The militarisation of the uprising

The resort to arms, while originally undertaken as necessary for the protection of peaceful demonstrations coming under regime fire, has taken on a central role as the goals, calculations and composition of an increasingly fragmented opposition have evolved. The escalation of the repression throughout the summer of 2011, with security sweeps around Damascus and military operations in Deraa, Hama and the province of Idlib, brought the question of the militarisation of the uprising to the fore. By early 2012, the armed struggle became a defining, dominant and irreversible feature of the Syrian uprising, even if peaceful demonstrations and civil disobedience continued to take place in parallel to armed action.

Early on, the wisdom and merits of militarisation provoked controversy and debate within the ranks of the opposition. Many activists who spearheaded the popular mobilisation and some domestic opposition groups, like the increasingly marginal NCC, feared that resorting to arms would cost the revolution the moral high ground; play to the advantage of a militarily stronger regime; radicalise the movement; shift power from civilian activists and politicians to armed commanders; put at risk and antagonise the population; cause immense material destruction and the collapse of state institutions; and create an opening for foreign involvement, including for jihadi fighters looking for a cause in the Arab world.

Ultimately, however, escalating repression by government forces, differing strategies within the opposition, the necessity of self-defence and a growing security vacuum overtook moral and strategic concerns about the resort to arms. The case for militarisation was further bolstered by the sense that international intervention was unlikely and diplomacy unable to end the crisis. The siege of the rebellious neighbourhood of Baba Amr in Homs in the winter of 2011–12, defended by small units of defectors and civilian combatants against a massive government onslaught, crystallised that shift and forced budding opposition groups to plan for a long military struggle. Even then, militarisation took many forms depending on local circumstances – while many rural towns saw the formation of local armed groups, cities saw an influx of non-resident fighters.

The Free Syrian Army (FSA)

The formation of armed rebel units, often driven by local dynamics, began in a chaotic and uncoordinated manner. Defectors, having left the regular military often out of revulsion at orders to open fire on demonstrators, provided the recruits for the early rebel units. Their ranks, therefore, largely comprised conscripts and low-level recruits from the regular military rather than from elite troops, and were overwhelmingly of Sunni origin. Civilian combatants, many of whom had honed basic fighting skills during conscription, quickly supplemented defector ranks, at first for self-defence purposes. Yet, it is notable that, initially, the fiercest fighting occurred in regions that were prime purveyors of army recruits, especially in Idlib and Deraa. Small numbers of officers and recruits formed loosely organised squads in these areas – as well as along the Lebanese and Turkish borders – and mostly conducted hit-and-run operations against loyalist forces.

The FSA emerged in 2011 as the nominal umbrella organisation of rebel groups. Turkey's proximity and early willingness to accommodate deserters proved crucial to its rise as defectors who formed the nucleus of the FSA in the summer of 2011 found sanctuary there. While constantly monitoring them, Turkish military intelligence allowed the rebels to organise in refugee camps and maintain contact with rebels inside Syria, and ignored the smuggling of weapons. Later, defectors also based themselves in

Jordan, where they received Jordanian assistance and developed their own funding and supply networks.

The FSA's leadership was keen on maintaining the pretence of a professional military force. In reality, from its inception, it was beset with structural problems. Its credibility and effectiveness suffered from a relatively junior leadership, weak control over units and operations, meagre resources, and the rapid proliferation of armed groups. Membership in the FSA entailed no obligation to follow its nominal leadership, but created often unmet expectations of support in unit commanders. To address concerns about the conduct of armed rebels, who often committed abuses, the FSA announced its respect of international war norms, including the Geneva Convention, but could not enforce this. Furthermore, reconciling the defectors' military culture with the behaviour of the civilian combatants and later of Islamist fighters proved immensely complicated: the former's emphasis on discipline and attempts to woo their former comrades clashed with the latter's risk-taking propensity and suspicions about those with former ties to the regime.[11]

Newly defected senior officers were willing to challenge the more junior leadership of the FSA: generals like Mustafa al-Sheikh and Mohamad Hajj Ali defied the leadership of Colonel Riad al-Asaad, the first FSA leader. They were later marginalised by a new cadre of senior officers from the provincial MCs and the SMC. Divisions at the top hampered efforts at unifying the rebellion, but tellingly had little impact on ground operations given how little control the leadership actually exerted.

The FSA, in its various incarnations, proved unable to manage the militarisation of the conflict and by extension the organisation and operations of rebel units. It depended on a streamlined foreign supply of weaponry to shore up its Turkey-based command, cultivate loyalty and impose discipline over Syria-based units. However, the failure of the SNC to mobilise resources and the funding biases of the Syrian diaspora and the

Gulf undercut this goal. Units nominally under the FSA umbrella developed their own supply networks. More importantly, in parallel with a thriving black market, much of the weaponry that fuelled the conflict was available or acquired locally: defectors fled with their arms, regime caches and barracks were raided, corrupt officers sold arsenals, workshops produced ammunitions and rockets. This further complicated the efforts of the FSA command to inject discipline and exercise control.

The rebel groups' growth in numbers and size and the spread of the fighting overtook the capacity of the leadership of the FSA. By mid-2012, estimates of defectors ranged from 30,000–60,000. The number of civilian combatants and foreign fighters is even more difficult to estimate. The ICRC's index of armed groups recorded as many as 1,000 operating in Syria by late 2012, of which only around half proclaimed their adherence to the FSA.[12]

These rebel groups varied in size, composition, organisation, reach and performance. Among the most effective were: the Farouq brigade, a large unit with a mildly Islamist orientation that operated mostly around Homs, Idlib and along the Turkish border; the Tawheed brigade, an Islamist group that led the fight into and around Aleppo; the Shuhada Suriya brigade, a collection of Sunni conservative but not ideological factions operating in Jabal al-Zawiyah and recruiting locally; Liwa al-Islam, an Islamist unit operating principally in the south and around Damascus; Ahrar al-Sham, a corps of Syrian Salafi fighters; and Jabhat al-Nusra (JN), a jihadi group composed of Syrian and foreign fighters. Many smaller battalions of secular-nationalist orientation operated alongside these larger units. Most rebel groups had local or regional ambitions, focused on the liberation of proximate territory, but Ahrar al-Sham and JN in particular have operated nationally.

The concurrent expansion, strengthening and fragmentation of the rebellion foreshadowed the prospect of warlordism and jihadism. This prompted a shift toward the establishment of MCs in each province that began in the spring of 2012. The MCs brought together high-ranking military defectors and civilian commanders. The initial impetus was to organise the local allocation of resources (including money), to coordinate operations at a provincial level, to bypass what was seen as a discredited and ineffective FSA command, and also to facilitate nationwide communication. The MCs included many of the secular and nationalist rebel units while several Islamist groups declined to join. The effectiveness of the MCs varied considerably: in Aleppo, other rebel groups like Tawheed bypassed it; the Deraa MC, largely based out of Jordan, benefitted from links to Jordanian, Saudi and, indirectly, US intelligence; and the Idlib MC struggled to impose its authority over well-resourced rebel units. Compounding these problems was external competition over the various FSA bodies, especially between Qatar and Saudi Arabia.[13] In the autumn of 2012, the former hosted several meetings of rebel commanders, prompting the latter to sponsor the Five Fronts Command.

Following the establishment of the NC in November 2012, the expectation of imminent foreign funding prompted an effort to bring greater coherence to the MCs. Under Turkish auspices and in the presence of Western and Arab military and intelligence officials, several hundreds of rebel commanders met in Antalya in December to form the SMC headed by General Salim Idriss. This defused, if only temporarily, tensions between Qatari- and Saudi-sponsored commanders.

Other rebel alliances, sometimes operationally more viable, operated alongside the SMC. The Syrian Islamic Front was formed in early 2013 and brought together home-grown Salafi factions, most notably Ahrar al-Sham, Liwa al-Haq and Suqoor al-Sham.[14] The Syrian Islamic Liberation Front, a looser and ideologically more moderate Islamist coalition, had formed in mid-2012; though it includes powerful units such as Farouq and Tawheed, it has less operational heft. The jihadi JN remained outside such arrangements to preserve its operational autonomy but also out of ideological purity.

Funding and weaponry

The organisation and military performance of the various rebel groups differed considerably depending on their access to weaponry and funding. Rebel groups seized their small and light weaponry mostly from regime arsenals or bought them on the black market. Until mid-2012, there was little evidence they had access to heavy weaponry or mechanised and armoured capabilities. Reports and anecdotal evidence from Syria indicate that foreign-sourced weapons accounted for no more than 15% of their total arsenal.[15] Better quality weaponry, such as anti-tank and anti-aircraft missiles, high-powered rifles and rockets, came from foreign sources but in small quantities.[16] Rebels set up workshops to produce their own Improvised Explosive Devices (IEDs), grenades and ammunition. They also seized armoured vehicles but not in sufficient numbers or with the adequate expertise to engage in conventional combat.[17]

Attracting foreign funding required rebel groups to develop an identity and their own patronage networks. Through social media, including YouTube and Facebook, rebel groups broadcast messages and showcased their successes, sometimes inflating them. Several groups have a multitude of funders and change identity accordingly.[18] For example, many have taken on an Islamist identity to appeal to conservative audiences abroad receptive to providing funding, especially in the Gulf states. Consequently, ascertaining the political affiliation or ideological orientation of every armed group has become a difficult task.

Much of the funding came from the Syrian diaspora based in the Gulf and Western countries. The existing fundraising networks of the MB in Saudi Arabia, Kuwait and Qatar outmatched those of newly established groups. In the US, the Syrian Support Group, an NGO set-up specifically to support the Syrian rebels, dealt exclusively with MCs, which were considered by the US government as moderate and therefore more acceptable rebel bodies. However, the length of the conflict and growing funding needs have put a strain on the diaspora;[19] its ability to provide sustained backing has been compounded by legal restrictions and the desire of governments to control funding streams.

A key factor determining rebel performance was the steadiness of supply and quality of weaponry. The rebel campaign in Aleppo almost drew to a halt in August 2012 when Tawheed and other groups ran out of ammunition, provoking internal disputes. Deraa's Jordan-based MC received weaponry and military advice as it prepared to confront Assad's forces ahead of a drive on Damascus, but Jordan's concerns about the rise of jihadis and problems with its own MB in the autumn of 2012 led to a pause in that assistance. By late 2012, the same rebel units around Deraa benefitted from a Saudi push to provide quality Croatian weaponry with Jordanian logistical assistance: this led to a series of rebel victories in strategic areas in the south, including along key highways linking Damascus to the border with Jordan.

The rebel military strategies

The absence of a unified rebel command and lack of communication impeded the definition of any nationwide strategy and objectives that would govern rebel military actions. Instead, uncoordinated initiatives, tactical opportunism, local entrepreneurship, misguided decisions and bravado shaped rebel actions at first. Equipped with small and light weaponry stolen from military arsenals or acquired on a thriving black market, rebel units opted for guerrilla tactics, conducting hit-and-run operations, attacking checkpoints and patrols and seizing government facilities. Rebels facilitated the movement of defectors across the country and the gathering of intelligence, as well as the supply of weaponry but also medical supplies and other essential goods.

By late 2011, the number of defections had grown considerably across the country, with many defectors seeking refuge in the province of Idlib, Jabal al-Zawiyah along the Turkish border, areas north of Aleppo and in the vicinity of Damascus. This rate of defection along with better local intelligence allowed for coordinated attacks on a variety of government facilities where weaponry was held: checkpoints, intelligence buildings, small military bases, Ba'ath Party centres and prisons.

The first large-scale military encounter took place in the city of Homs, from October to November 2011. The battle of Baba Amr, a dense and poor Sunni neighbourhood, demonstrated the strategic and tactical confusion of the rebels at that time. The location of Homs on the highway from Damascus to Aleppo and the coastal regions, as well as its large Alawite population, made its control a strategic imperative for the regime. The presence of large numbers of defectors and the fears of Sunni residents about impending massacres led to a decision to make a stand in this populous urban setting.

Later, a strategic veneer was added: the resistance of Baba Amr would force the hand of the international community and would galvanise the rest of the country. Despite outrage at the scale of destruction, these goals were not attained: the Arab League and UN efforts were in their initial phases, no government showed appetite for intervention, and while Baba Amr's suffering roused protesters, it did not lead to a general insurrection. An incessant and indiscriminate barrage of artillery and a blockade eventually forced the rebels to leave the neighbourhood, mainly through secret tunnels that served for resupply and evacuations.

The defeat in Baba Amr forced a revision in strategy, towards a war of attrition in the countryside aimed at liberating ground for use as a safe haven and launching pad, breaking regime supply lines, disrupting its territorial continuity and seizing small and middle-sized bases. As part of its strategy of control, but also its defence posture, the Syrian regime had built small army bases across the country (many of which were air-defence installations in case of an Israeli attack, but there were also mid-sized airports and infantry barracks). Isolated and difficult to resupply, they proved to be easier targets for the rebels.

A key objective of the insurgents was to erode Assad's air dominance so as to shelter liberated areas. This air superiority prevented the organisation and training of large rebel units, while the terror and damage inflicted by fixed- and rotary-wing capabilities often alienated civilians from rebels, as their presence was blamed for attacks.

Once it became clear that rebel demands for a no-fly zone and later for anti-aircraft missiles would not be met, alternative strategies were adopted: the use of anti-aircraft missiles stolen from government arsenals and direct attacks on air bases, most notably in the north. For example, the Taftanaz air base in the Idlib province, which hosted two dozen helicopters and sat in the middle of rebel-held territory along the Wadi Deif front, was overrun in January 2013. Seizing major bases forced rebel units to agree on tactical cooperation and the pooling of man- and fire-power. The siege and capture of Taftanaz involved units from Farouq, Shuhada Suriya, Ahrar al-Sham and JN brigades. The capture of Aleppo's infantry school, known as al-Mushat, in December 2012 was mainly the doing of the Tawheed brigades, with assistance from smaller factions.[20]

The rebels also seized border points with Turkey (notably Tal Abyad and Bab al-Hawa by Farouq in September 2012 and Ras al-Ayn by a motley of rebel groups) and Iraq to facilitate supply and movement of refugees and fighters. Minefields and army deployments along the Lebanese border complicated smuggling routes there: while Lebanon's northern border, and especially the Wadi Khaled area, was effectively shut off, the cities of Ersal and al-Qaa provided weaponry and a safe haven to Syrian rebels fighting southwest of Homs.

By late 2012, the FSA and Islamist brigades (including Liwa al-Islam) had set the capture of Damascus as an objective. They launched a move to squeeze loyalist forces from the south, gain control of the highways into Jordan and gather forces in the south and east of the capital. The rebels' strategic rationale was that confronting Assad in the capital would force him to abandon the rest of the country and concentrate his forces there. Assad had, however, amassed his elite troops and considerable artillery and air power in the defence of the capital, and proceeded to clear out Damascus's vicinity, razing the town of Daraya, a hotbed of resistance near to a vital military airport.

The significance of the battle for Aleppo

Despite successes across the countryside, by early 2013 rebel groups had not yet captured a major city. Internal divisions, insufficient capabilities, deficient operational and logistical coordination, but also complex urban terrains and resolute government resistance accounted for that failure.

The most significant example of rebel overreach occurred in Aleppo in the summer of 2012. Up until then, rebels had led a war of attrition, primarily aimed at harassing and degrading government forces in the surrounding rural areas. A sense of rebel momentum, born from the successful capture of much of the countryside around the city, prompted rebel units, including the large Tawheed and Suqoor al-Sham brigades, to attempt to seize the city. The strategic rationale was compelling: victory in the country's largest city would have created a rebel-controlled zone extending to the Turkish border.

The campaign, expected by rebel commanders to be swift, proved long, costly, uncertain and politically damaging as it transformed into urban warfare and froze into a stalemate. It was complicated by the city's diverse sectarian and ethnic composition. The offensive was launched with little consultation with other rebel units and the Aleppo MC and suffered from inadequate preparation, causing battlefield frictions between commanders over objectives and tactics. Having planned for a short operation, units also encountered supply problems, running short of ammunition and weaponry at crucial moments. At the operational level, rebel units displayed deficient tactical coordination, but also competition. By late 2012, the fighting had split the city: rebel units controlled the south and north-east of the city and loyalist forces held on to the rest (including the main airport) and mounted counter-attacks. Ominously, members of minority groups organised in response to the rebel advance. Kurdish factions seized several neighbourhoods while Christians armed themselves for self-protection, some joining regime ranks.

The absence of a political-military strategy was reflected by the lack of significant political mobilisation in support of the rebel operation inside the city, although there were signs of dissent among lawyers, students and professional classes in the preceding months. Early human-rights abuses against regime supporters (notably the public execution of the leaders of the Berri clan), enduring urban-rural tensions, the collapse of order, severe food and medical shortages and rebel indiscipline (including instances of looting, arbitrary arrests and executions) alienated many inhabitants.

The fighting inflicted considerable human loss and destruction, including to the historic parts of the city; it also caused a major refugee crisis. It exposed crucial rebel shortcomings, including the absence of local political authority and of mechanisms of accountability, and helped Islamist groups make political and military inroads. It eroded the image of the revolutionaries politically, and foreboded a potentially bloodier and more destructive fight over Damascus, better defended and strategically more vital for the Assad regime.

The challenge of governance and relief

The capture of territory by rebel units shifted responsibility for local administration and humanitarian assistance onto their shoulders. The process of establishing governance and security and of providing essential goods and services to the population was fraught with difficulties. The issue of governance became a key test of the credibility of the rebels and their political patrons. Given its shrinking resources and the fact that its priorities lay elsewhere, the regime seemed satisfied to pass that burden onto its unprepared and under-resourced opponents.

Models of local administration varied considerably, depending on local conditions, the identity and performance of the controlling rebel group, the availability of resources and the existence of administrative capacity. In some places, institutions were preserved to keep local life running after local bureaucrats shifted sides, as happened in much of Idlib. In others, local leaders and civilian activists took charge, establishing courts and humanitarian bodies. Elsewhere, armed groups imposed their own authority over sometimes noncompliant populations, with varying levels of success. Tensions between local activists and Islamist fighters in the Sunni town of Saraqeb escalated after the former challenged the latter's attempt to impose more Islamist social norms. In several places, the attempt by Islamist factions, including JN, to replace the three-starred Syrian revolutionary flag with their Islamist black banners was met with disapproval and protests.

The magnitude of the humanitarian situation and the management of scarce resources often overwhelmed rebel capacity. Ominously, rebel fighters had, at times, behaved as predators in Aleppo and elsewhere, looting private property and businesses, engaging in vigilante justice, crimes and abuses, and alienating the local population by expecting preferential treatment.[21] In comparison, JN enforced discipline on its fighters and distributed food and other essential goods, gaining support particularly in Aleppo and northern parts of Syria.

Revolution and Islamism

Unsurprisingly, for a country with an overwhelming Sunni majority, the various strains of Sunni political Islam have profoundly shaped the character and trajectory of the uprising and the civil war. In particular, the rise of jihadism proved to be the Assad regime's most troubling self-fulfilling prophecy.

To weaken the grip of Islamist organisations, the Syrian state had pursued a strategy of co-optation of Sunni clerical networks and tight control of the Waqf (the official Sunni endowment system). As the Ba'ath Party lost ideological appeal, the regime cultivated influential mainstream clerical figures, often of Sufi persuasion, as conduits into Syrian society.[22] These included Sheikh Ahmad Kaftaro, Sheikh Ahmed Badreddine Hassoun (an Aleppine cleric who became Syria's grand mufti and a loyal Assad supporter), Sheikh Mohammed Habbash (a cleric who purportedly represented a modernist brand of Islam and who entered parliament but later defected), and Sheikh Said Ramadan al-Butti (a senior preacher in Damascus). It also allowed religious networks such as the *qubaysiyat* movement which enrolled middle-class Sunni women for social work. The Assad family itself publicly adopted Sunni Islam in official rituals, and both Bashar and Maher married into Sunni families. This pretence served to balance the official secularism of the ruling party and state with the more conservative nature of Syrian society.

Similar to other Arab societies, Syria's has become more pious and conservative since the 1970s, the result of disenchantment with the failure of secular pan-Arab nationalist ideologies, authoritarian rule and a desire to assert identity. This was expressed through more religious personal and social behaviours, including public displays of religiosity, and is a trend that clashed with the avowed secular nature of the Syrian state, leading to tense adaptations and compromises. The rise of Islamism throughout the Arab world was profoundly problematic for the Assad family, which worried that its legitimacy would be questioned on religious grounds. But it was also useful in framing choices: to both internal and external audiences, the regime portrayed itself as the only alternative to Islamism, however loosely defined.

Syria has been shaken by several episodes of Islamist violence since its independence, most notably during the 1976–82 period. Spearheaded by the Sunni MB, supported by segments of the Sunni population that had lost power and standing because of the Ba'ath's economic and social policies, this struggle against the Assad regime had a profoundly sectarian character. As a result, it was narrowly based and failed to mobilise society. The MB-led rebellion in Hama ended in failure after the Assad regime razed the city in February 1982, and many Syrians blamed the two sides equally.

Compared to its Egyptian counterpart, the MB had little presence left in society by the time the uprising started. Its leadership operated in exile and membership in the organisation was punishable by death. It could not run for elections, did not have representatives in professional bodies, could not be involved in charity work or overtly control mosques. Importantly, many Syrians simply distrusted it for its history of violence and its failed political ventures (such as the short-lived venture in 2006 with Abdel-Halim Khaddam). The MB itself was spread across several branches, and was divided over political strategy: the Aleppo branch of Ali Bayanouni, the organisation's leader until 2010, is more political and open to other opposition groups, while the Hama branch of Mohammed Riad al-Shaqfeh, his successor, is more purist and politically rigid.

The absence of the MB created an opening for loosely organised but better funded Salafi groups. The emergence of Salafism benefitted from several factors: the exposure of Syrian expatriates in the Arabian Peninsula to the more austere Wahhabi brand of Islam; the tribal and other links between Syria and the Gulf states; and indoctrination of Syrian clerics in Gulf-funded religious institutions. From 2003, the proximity of Iraq and the repercussions of its civil war added complexity. In a bid to gain influence next door and pressure the US, Syria allowed foreign jihadi fighters to use and transit through its territory to enter Iraq so as to fight the US occupation and partake in Iraq's sectarian war. While carefully monitored and often manipulated by Syrian intelligence, these fighters benefitted from support networks inside Syria and grew in size and prominence. The defeat of al-Qaeda in Iraq (AQI) at the hands of Sunni tribal fighters (the Awakening or Sahwa movement), US forces and the Iraqi army created a cadre of unemployed, frustrated and available fighters.

Islamist revolutionary mobilisation
In comparison with previous bouts of unrest, Syria's current uprising initially appeared rooted in dissatisfaction that was not primarily religious in character and driven by elements of society that did not identify primarily or solely by sect. As in Tunisia and Egypt, it came as a surprise to Islamist movements and clerical figures. Co-opted by the regime, risk-averse or simply unconvinced, many Sunni religious leaders initially showed little of the courage and creativity displayed by the mostly secular activists belonging to grassroots networks. Fearing regime retaliation, many at first refused the use of their mosques and religious centres for demonstrations. Several regime-aligned clerics, such as al-Butti, made speeches denouncing the uprising and demanding loyalty to the ruler; others, like al-Khatib who rose to become the head of the NC, provided religious cover for the democratic demands of the revolution and denounced the crackdown.[23] In small towns and rural areas, mosques became the rallying points for demonstrators. As the death toll of protesters grew, funerals and commemorations provided momentum for ever more revolutionary mobilisation.

However caught off guard Islamist networks were to begin with, they quickly embraced the revolution and became central players in both its peaceful and violent dimensions.[24] As the uprising grew in complexity and magnitude, local clerics and national organisations proved able to leverage local networks, fundraise abroad, attract media attention and infuse a sense of purpose and identity in the movement. The complex process of radicalisation, fed by despair and sectarian mobilisation, found its ultimate expression in the rise of Salafism.

Indeed, the absence of a clear and credible opposition leadership in the early days of the uprising allowed media-savvy foreign-based and sometimes non-Syrian clerics to inject poisonous geopolitical and sectarian narratives that were partially corroborated by the regime's response. One such cleric who managed to instigate sectarian mobilisation is Sheikh Adnan al-Arour, a Syrian cleric based in Saudi Arabia; his frequent appearances on Al-Wesal, a sectarian Saudi-owned TV station, and his use of social media, built him a nominal following among rebels and oppositionists eager to inscribe the struggle into a broader context. In reality, his following on the ground appears to be small. His denunciations of Alawites and other regime supporters contributed to the minorities' distrust of the revolutionary movement.

Islamist groups, whether home-grown or foreign-inspired, have had to face a guarded and diverse Syrian society. The Assad regime uniformly painted them as dangerous fundamentalists bent on imposing sharia rule and discrimination against non-Sunni communities. They did indeed harbour fundamentalist, including foreign, elements who grew more vocal and assertive as the struggle acquired a greater sectarian character. Even among conservative Sunni constituencies, Salafi jihadi factions had to tread carefully given the damage and pain they caused to neighbouring Iraqi society.

Moreover, Islamist movements operating in Syria were fragmented: the spectrum ranges from groups that preach social conservatism but prefer to separate religion from politics, like

Farouq, to ones that advocate the establishment of an Islamist state, like Tawheed, to some that subscribe to jihadi ideology, with or without global reach, like, respectively, JN and Ahrar al-Sham.

It is difficult to ascertain the power and cohesiveness of each Islamist faction, as their size, financial strength, local presence and foreign patronage vary considerably. Backed by Qatar and Turkey, and with a strong base in the diaspora, the MB has been able to flex its muscles within the political opposition. Thanks to better financing, it has been able to build a presence inside Syria and relations with major rebel brigades, like Tawheed and Farouq, but has also attempted to form its own armed branch.[25]

The MB's influence within Syrian society is difficult to evaluate; the movement is constrained by its indispensable alliances with secular forces and its external relationships. By comparison, the Salafi factions are fragmented and loosely organised, their ideology fluid, their funding opaque and their foreign patrons divided and not necessarily able to influence their behaviour.

Not all clerics emerged as sectarian entrepreneurs: in many places, Syria's own tradition of Sunni moderation and history of religious coexistence prevailed over sectarian instincts and helped ensure social order and governance as the state faded. Traditional clerics are more established and respected in society, but they have long operated under the umbrella of the state and have meagre resources. Comparatively poor and less able to protect their people, such moderate figures have suffered from the radicalisation of the conflict.

The rise of Islamist militias
The radicalisation of the conflict starting in the second half of 2011 provided willing home-grown recruits and foreign funding, but it also offered foreign jihadi fighters a cause to fight for in the heart of the Levant. Well-funded and organised, more disciplined and promoting an ideological vision that gives purpose

to the suffering and sacrifice, armed Islamist movements have undoubtedly developed an edge over the less-structured secular opposition movements organised under the FSA umbrella.

From the jihadi-takfiri perspective – that seeks to impose a harsh, puritan Islamic state and considers non-Sunni communities as either inferior in terms of rights (Christians, for example) or heretical (Shia, for example) – the struggle in Syria pits a disenfranchised Sunni majority against an oppressive heretic Alawite minority, itself backed by Shia Iran. It provides an opportunity to reverse the defeat in Iraq against the Shia-dominated government and perhaps even rekindle the fight there. The struggle in Syria could revive global jihadism after a series of ideological and military setbacks in previous years, and a victory, however defined, would give these groups a prime base of operations in the Levant. In February 2012, Ayman Zawahiri, the leader of al-Qaeda, called for such jihadi mobilisation against Assad's 'pernicious, cancerous regime'.[26] Surfing on the revolutionary wave, Zawahiri adopted seemingly progressive language: 'If we want freedom, we must be liberated from this regime. If we want justice, we must retaliate against this regime. Continue your revolt and anger, don't accept anything else apart from independent, respectful governments.'[27]

Indeed, the conflict in Syria created new opportunities for foreign fighters. A few thousand veterans of the wars in Iraq, Afghanistan, Chechnya and the Balkans flocked into Syria, mostly to form distinct combat units.[28] As of late 2012, estimates of foreign fighters hovered around 3,000–5,000,[29] while homegrown Salafis joined them or formed their own battalions. Of course not all are motivated by jihadi ideology or approve of takfiri tenets; many Libyan fighters have joined out of revolutionary solidarity after overthrowing Gadhafi.[30]

Cohabitation between Islamist militias and FSA brigades has proved tense: the religious and ideological perspective of the former clashes with the nationalist and revolutionary outlook of the latter, especially those composed of military defectors. Zeal, discipline and resources further differentiates them, creating resentment and competition. The embrace by local populations of extreme Islamist factions was neither ideological nor absolute; rather it has been driven by opportunism, despair and necessity.

Most prominent among jihadi groups is the shadowy JN, whose first-known attacks were car and suicide bombings in Damascus and Aleppo in early 2012. Composed mostly of foreign fighters, including Jordanians and Iraqis, and toughened veterans of the Iraq war, JN has demonstrated a mix of fighting skills, ruthlessness and discipline, ranking it among the best performing rebel units. As a formidable fighting force, it has played a crucial role in the capture of key military installations, such as the Sheikh Suleiman and Taftanaz bases, as well as in the defence of key Aleppo districts and the capture of parts of the surrounding countryside. It has also proven adaptable to the terrain over which it fights: it behaved as a guerrilla force in Aleppo while it deployed terrorist tactics in Damascus. JN has conducted an effective communications campaign, broadcasting videos of its operations and victories in a bid to heighten its profile and attract funding.[31] As a result, small rebel units have sought to join JN. In December 2012, however, the US listed JN as a foreign terrorist organisation for its links with AQI and terrorist tactics. The death in combat of a close relative of the slain AQI leader Abu Musab al-Zarqawi, in early 2013, appeared to validate the US assessment.[32]

Alongside JN, many other Islamist brigades operate, the largest and most prominent of which are Ahrar al-Sham and Suqoor al-Sham. Both have attracted home-grown Salafis and have largely shunned terrorist tactics, such as suicide attacks. They have also developed a local presence across the country, administering several liberated areas. When several dozen Islamist groups formed the Syrian Islamic Front, including Ahrar al-Sham and Suqoor al-Sham, significantly JN did not join.[33] This was further evidence of JN's desire to establish an independent identity as a vanguard group and to preserve its operational autonomy – only collaborating with other units on specific operations.

The performance and discipline of jihadi outfits has caused political complications for the mainstream opposition, represented by the SNC and NC, as Islamist factions have, at times, posed a direct challenge. In a November 2012 video statement, Islamist commanders from several non-FSA groups in Aleppo denounced the formation of the NC and its pluralistic platform, calling instead for 'the establishment of a just Islamic state'.[34] Later, under pressure from their foreign backers and after being lambasted by the Aleppo MC and revolutionary activists, several factions recanted this declaration. The damage was done, however: the call strengthened suspicions that fundamentalist factions would push an Islamist agenda quietly, if not forcefully, and create de facto Islamist governance in areas they controlled.

While not subscribing to the extreme ideology of Salafi organisations, the political opposition has had to acknowledge their significant military contribution to the struggle against Assad. After the US listing of JN as a foreign terrorist organisation, the NC felt compelled to dissociate itself from the US decision. The backlash against the designation of JN also extended to other rebel factions and opposition sympathisers who saw Assad, rather than jihadi groups, as the prime source of threat. These reactions and the growth of Salafi groups has further complicated the NC's crucial yet muddled outreach to already apprehensive minorities and made its promises of a pluralistic post-Assad order sound hollow. Meanwhile, the Assad regime and its foreign allies appear vindicated in highlighting the rise of Salafism.

The emergence of factions with extremist outlooks has also threatened the prospects for foreign backing. Concerns have centred on whether they would seize chemical weapons from

Assad's arsenal, operate provocatively along the border with Israel or use Syrian soil to destabilise Jordan, Lebanon and Iraq. Western states denied rebels sophisticated weaponry, including anti-aircraft missiles, precisely to avoid any leakage to jihadi groups. Consequently, the US has made its support contingent on their isolation and firm rejection by the political opposition. Turkey, which has reluctantly facilitated the funding and arming of rebel factions, still considers the Salafi growth on its immediate borders a threat. The Gulf states, especially Saudi Arabia and Kuwait, have appeared ambivalent: their influence in Syria owes much to these groups that benefitted from Gulf funding; at the same time, these organisations could turn against their funders and pose potent ideological and security threats, as has happened before.

At the time of writing, Salafi groups remain popular because they are better disciplined and organised. In several cities, they have provided humanitarian assistance, imposed order and prevented looting and abuses; FSA units have fared poorly in comparison. Despite many instances of imposition of their more conservative social mores (for example the destruction of liquor stocks), they have, to date, refrained from applying harsh sharia law on liberated territories, perhaps to avoid early stigmatisation and the backlash suffered when AQI did so. When they have sought to impose this, they have often met with resistance from local activists and civilians, in towns such as Saraqeb.

However, the prospect of clashes between mainstream FSA units and jihadis appears plausible in the medium term. Jihadi groups have no committed foreign patrons, and their usefulness in the fight against Assad is balanced by the societal damage they could cause and their threat to regional stability. Their hardline ideology, terrorist tactics and lack of nationalist commitment could well alienate significant segments of Syrian society. To convince fence-sitters and minorities to shift loyalty away from Assad, the political opposition and its armed allies will have to contain the jihadi menace. Indeed, jihadi groups may emerge as a formidable obstacle to a political transition and the adoption of a new, inclusive political order. Already, several incidents have put jihadis and rebels in opposition to one another. For example, in April 2012, FSA rebels in the town of Qusayr killed Said al-Boustani, a Lebanese jihadi leader of Fatah al-Islam. However, the most serious such incident was the shooting of Firas al-Absi, a JN leader, in September 2012, followed by the retaliatory killing of Thaer al-Waqqas, a commander of the Farouq brigade. The two commanders had fought over the control of the important border point of Bab al-Hawa.

In summary, the political and structural weakness of Syria's political opposition and the rise of a multitude of rebel groups significantly complicate their shared objective of ousting Assad. The belief among rebel commanders that a military victory is possible and desirable comes at the cost of a more subtle political posture aimed at fracturing Assad's support base through incentives and guarantees. The mutation of Syria's uprising into a zero-sum civil war has probably neutered any such political strategy.

Notes

[1] Full text of the Damascus Declaration available in English at: *Syria Comment*, 1 November 2005, http://faculty-staff.ou.edu/L/Joshua.M.Landis-1/syriablog/2005/11/damascus-declaration-in-english.htm.

[2] 'Syria: Harsh Sentence for Prominent Rights Lawyer', *Human Rights Watch*, 25 April 2007, http://www.hrw.org/news/2007/04/24/syria-harsh-sentence-prominent-rights-lawyer.

[3] Pierret, 'The role of the mosque in the Syrian revolution', *Near East Quarterly*, 20 March 2012, http://www.neareastquarterly.com/index.php/2012/03/20/the-role-of-the-mosque-in-the-syrian-revolution/.

[4] 'The Syrian National Initiative', *Carnegie Middle East Center*, 1 November 2012, http://carnegie-mec.org/publications/?fa=49872.

[5] MacFarquhar and Micheal R. Gordon, 'As Fighting Rages, Clinton Seeks New Syrian Opposition', *The New York Times*, 31 October 2012, http://www.nytimes.com/2012/11/01/world/middleeast/syrian-air-raids-increase-as-battle-for-

strategic-areas-intensifies-rebels-say.html?_r=0.

6 'Moaz al-Khatib: letter to the Christians of Syria', *Carnegie Middle East Center*, 1 January 2013, http://carnegie-mec.org/publications/?fa=50728.

7 'Moaz al-Khatib yurid 3 miliarat dular li-ta'sis hukuma intiqaliyya', YouTube, 24 January 2013, http://youtu.be/5gCa9Ir_2DE.

8 'Group Denial: Repression of Kurdish Political and Cultural Rights in Syria', *Human Rights Watch*, 26 November 2009, http://www.hrw.org/sites/default/files/reports/syria1109web_0.pdf.

9 'Burhan Ghalioun: There is no such thing as Syrian Kurdistan', *Rudaw*, 17 April 2012, http://www.kurdnas.com/en/index.php?option=com_content&view=article&id=449:burhan-ghalioun-there-is-no-such-thing-as-syrian-kurdistan&catid=3:newsflash&Itemid=54.

10 Lauren Williams, 'Inter-Kurdish tensions mounting against FSA', *The Daily Star*, 20 November 2012, http://www.dailystar.com.lb/News/Middle-East/2012/Nov-20/195610-inter-kurdish-tensions-mounting-against-fsa.ashx#axzz2IRvWXxue.

11 'Syria: FSA's Statement about Geneva Convention for Treating Prisoners', YouTube, 2 August 2012, https://www.youtube.com/watch?v=NxWyIeEgtMg.

12 Email exchange with senior humanitarian official, and reported conversation with ICRC official, Davos, February 2013, https://twitter.com/chipmanj/status/295155812593197057.

13 'Syria's Secular and Islamist Rebels: Who Are the Saudis and the Qataris Arming?', *Time Magazine*, 18 September 2012, http://world.time.com/2012/09/18/syrias-secular-and-islamist-rebels-who-are-the-saudis-and-the-qataris-arming/.

14 See the Facebook page for the Islamic Syrian Front: https://www.facebook.com/Islamic.Syrian.Front/posts/136004689894218.

15 Interview with rebel commander, Antakya, April 2012.

16 Interview with French security official, Paris, October 2012.

17 Interview with rebel commander, Maarat an-Nu'man (Syria), October 2012.

18 Abigail Fielding-Smith, 'Syria rebels exploit rivals' successes', *Financial Times*, 3 December 2012, http://www.ft.com/cms/s/0/5da95558-3d16-11e2-9e13-00144feabdc0.html#axzz2J1SmeSel.

19 Interviews with members of the Syrian diaspora, Doha, September 2012, and Dubai, November 2012.

20 'La chute d'Al-Mouchat', *Le Monde*, 6 January 2013.

21 'Syria: End Opposition Use of Torture, Executions', *Human Rights Watch*, 17 September 2012, http://www.hrw.org/news/2012/09/17/syria-end-opposition-use-torture-executions.

22 For an essential look at Syria's Sunni clerical milieu and its interaction with the Assad regime, see: Pierret, *Baas et Islam en Syrie. La dynastie Assad face aux oulémas* (Paris: PUF, 2011).

23 See: Pierret, 'The role of the mosque in the Syrian revolution'.

24 For a look at the diversity of Islamist trends in the early stages of the Syrian uprising, see: Pierret, 'Syrie: l'islam dans la revolution', *Politique étrangère*, vol. 76, no. 4, Hiver 2011, pp. 879–891.

25 Ruth Sherlock and Richard Spencer, 'Muslim Brotherhood establishes

militia inside Syria', *The Telegraph*, 3 August 2012, http://www. telegraph.co.uk/news/worldnews/ middleeast/syria/9450587/Muslim-Brotherhood-establishes-militia-inside-Syria.html.

26 Jason Burke, 'Al-Qaida leader Zawahiri urges Muslim support for Syrian uprising', *The Guardian*, 12 February 2012, http://www. guardian.co.uk/world/2012/feb/12/ alqaida-zawahiri-support-syrian-uprising.

27 *Ibid.*

28 Ghaith Abdul-Ahad, 'Syria: the foreign fighters joining the war against Bashar al-Assad', *The Guardian*, 23 September 2012, http:// www.guardian.co.uk/world/2012/ sep/23/syria-foreign-fighters-joining-war.

29 Interview with French official, Paris, October 2012.

30 Mary Fitzgerald, 'The Syrian rebels' Libyan Weapon', *Foreign Policy*, 9 August 2012, http://www.foreign policy.com/articles/2012/08/09/ the_syrian_rebels_libyan_weapon.

31 'Mu'assasat al-minara al-bayda tuqaddam: Halab … Ma'rakat al-'Ezz', YouTube, 13 December 2012, http://youtu.be/LBnMHnZBZzA.

32 'Zarqawi brother-in-law killed in Syria: Jordan Salafist', *The Daily Star*, 17 January 2013, http://www. dailystar.com.lb/News/Middle-East/2013/Jan-17/202659-zarqawi-brother-in-law-killed-in-syria-jordan-salafist.ashx.

33 Aaron Y. Zelin, 'The Syrian Islamic Front's Order of Battle', *al-Wasat*, 22 January 2013, http://thewasat. wordpress.com/2013/01/22/syrian-islamic-fronts-order-of-battle/.

34 See: 'Ajil: Kata'ib halab yarfudun al-i'tilaf wa yattafiqun 'ala ta'sis dawla islamiyya', a video posted on the Facebook page of the group 'Da'm tarshid wa tawjih al-thawra fi wijh nitham al-'abth al-suri', https://www.facebook.com/photo. php?v=113081425522913.

CHAPTER FOUR

The regional struggle over Syria

Syria in the regional landscape

On the eve of the Syrian uprising, the Assad regime was confident and assertive, having weathered considerable regional challenges. Its position had markedly improved after years of isolation, pressure and uncertainty. Relations with regional rivals had ameliorated at no apparent cost to its posture and strategic choices, and compared to other Arab leaders, Assad's popularity ranked second only to that of Hassan Nasrallah, Hizbullah's charismatic leader.[1]

Assad's position had reached its lowest point after the forced withdrawal of Syrian troops from Lebanon in the spring of 2005, following massive peaceful protests in Beirut and international accusations that Damascus orchestrated the assassination of the former Lebanese Prime Minister Rafik Hariri. However, a fast-changing regional landscape contributed to Assad's resurgence. The departure of US forces from Iraq, and with it the threat of US military pressure on Syria, compounded the vastly more accommodating tone of the Obama administration towards Damascus. The new US administration proved to be no longer willing to lead the camp that had ostracised Syria and was keen to explore ways to restart Israeli-Syrian peace talks. This new US approach contributed to altering the policies of states that had so far adopted a hardline position on Syria, especially Saudi Arabia.

To balance the influence of these countries, Assad had cunningly leveraged his rapidly developing relations with Turkey, a regional powerhouse, and the tiny, but ambitious and rich, Gulf state of Qatar. The coming to power of the moderate Islamist Justice and Development Party (AKP) altered the strategic posture of Ankara, which had until then prioritised relations with the West over its immediate Arab neighbourhood. As part of a re-energised Arab policy based on Turkish soft power and mercantile interests, the government of Recep Tayyip Erdogan pursued a spectacular rapprochement with Damascus starting in 2003. Bilateral relations had, until then, been antagonistic due to the dispute over Sanjak of Antioch (Turkey's Hatay province) and Syria's dealings with the armed separatist group, the PKK.

Having opposed the 2003 US invasion of Iraq and strengthened its ties with Iran, Hamas and Hizbullah, Turkey's entreaties were welcomed by Syria. The relationship flourished politically and economically. Turkish businesses flooded Syria with goods and invested in major projects, while the once quiet border became a bustling commercial route with bilateral trade reaching US$2.5bn in 2010.[2] Aleppo, Syria's economic centre, particularly profited, even as Syrian industry suffered from Turkish competition. Tourism and trans-border exchanges grew as visas were lifted in 2009. The relationship also had a security dimension: joint military exercises were held while the two countries developed intelligence cooperation.

As expected, Turkey provided significant cover for Syria. As a NATO member, Turkey could moderate the behaviour of Western states, mediate with them and provide a buffer if need be. Indeed, Erdogan repeatedly interceded on Assad's behalf with the US, the EU, Iraq and the Gulf states, and, significantly, facilitated secret, if ultimately inconclusive, peace talks between

Syria and Israel. Assad benefitted from associating with Erdogan, whose popularity in the Arab world stemmed from his bombastic criticism of Israel as well as Turkey's economic success. As a respected and successful Muslim state, Turkey could extend legitimacy and allay the perception of Syrian dependency on Iran. There was also a strong personal dimension to this relationship, with Assad and Erdogan striking up a friendship and vacationing together with their spouses. (Later, as the official relationship soured, both claimed to have been betrayed and manipulated.)

Despite divided opinion in Turkey over the country's orientation, Erdogan and Foreign Minister Ahmet Davutoglu, who had devised a policy known as 'zero problems with neighbors',[3] could show tangible results in Syria. This successful rapprochement became proof of the merits of this realignment, at a time when its relationship with the EU was fraying.

Qatar was another valued partner of Assad. The tiny Gulf state was charting a foreign policy often at odds with that of Saudi Arabia, the Arabian Peninsula's economic and political powerhouse. Buttressed by enormous wealth and, thanks to *al-Jazeera*, region-wide influence, Qatar's dynamic, agile and ambitious leadership sought to become a player and intermediary in several regional conflicts. Qatar maintained good relations with the US, the EU and, quietly, Israel. Importantly, the Qatari Emir Sheikh Hamad al-Thani shared with Assad a similar distrust of Saudi Arabia and good relations with Iran, albeit of differing scope and intensity.

Consequently, Qatari-owned companies invested heavily in Syrian real estate, tourism and infrastructure projects. This fitted in well with Syria's development strategy to encourage foreign investment and private sector employment but, ultimately, did not create the expected jobs. Moreover, Qatari and Gulf investment was primarily channelled through businessmen close to the regime, further aggravating corruption and inequalities.

To the despair of the Gulf states and Egypt, Syria's long-standing and force-multiplying alliance with Iran had become a defining feature of the Middle Eastern regional order. Saudi Arabia's primary goal had been to distance Syria from Iran, but attempts to pry Damascus away from Tehran failed in the face of their mutual commitment, US entanglement in Iraq and the military successes of their Lebanese and Palestinian allies, Hizbullah and Hamas, against Israel. Damascus was seen as the prime enabler of Iranian influence in the Levant and, as an Arab state, an embarrassing irritant to self-proclaimed Saudi leadership of the Arab world. As well as Syria's alliance with Iran and Hizbullah, its suspected role in the assassination of Hariri, a Saudi protégé, was also a key sticking point. As a result, Saudi Arabia sought to orchestrate Syria's isolation by, for instance, sending a low-level delegation to an Arab League summit held in Damascus in March 2008 and pressuring other states into downgrading their relations with Assad.

Qatari mediation over the Lebanese power struggle in 2008 and the conflict between Israel and Hamas in the Gaza strip in 2008–09 facilitated Syria's reintegration into the Arab fold. This culminated in the Saudi-Syrian rapprochement starting in 2009 over Lebanon, a country over which they had bitterly fought since 2005. In July 2010, King Abdullah of Saudi Arabia and Assad paid a joint visit to Beirut, during which Saad Hariri, the Lebanese prime minister and son of the assassinated leader, was asked to moderate his opposition to Assad and reconcile with Hizbullah. He was also told to distance himself from an international court set up to prosecute individuals implicated in the assassinations of anti-Assad Lebanese media and political figures.[4]

Even the relationship with Israel seemed stable. In Israeli eyes, Syria was a weak and predictable enemy, unwilling to escalate directly and easy to deter. As a result, Israel had avoided targeting Syria during and after the 2006 war against Hizbullah, despite evidence of massive Syrian logistical help and the fact that Damascus was seen as being able to constrain the Shia guerrilla organisation. After Israeli intelligence uncovered the existence of Syria's covert nuclear programme, the decision was taken to destroy the Kibar reactor in September 2007 but refrain from publicising the operation to limit the possibility that Syria would retaliate out of humiliation. Syrian authorities predictably maintained silence over that episode, as they did over the assassinations inside Syria of Hizbullah security chief Imad Mughniyeh and of General Muhammad Sleiman, a senior Syrian military official implicated in sensitive security matters. Only two months after the destruction of its nuclear programme, Syria participated in the Annapolis peace talks and entered peace talks with Israel through Turkish mediation.

Assad had also managed to restore Syrian influence in Lebanon through his allies there. While Syria was no longer able to dominate the Lebanese political game, its alignment of interests and similar strategic outlook with Hizbullah (now part of the Lebanese cabinet) meant it could thwart any move perceived as antagonistic to its interests. Hizbullah obstructed funding and government authorisation for the international tribunal and secured the position of Syrian allies inside the government, bureaucracy and security services. Later, as relations with European and Arab states improved, Syria was able to obtain significant returns for largely symbolic concessions, such as the establishment of formal diplomatic relations with Lebanon.

However, even as Assad rejoiced in his foreign-policy victories, Syria remained more a spoiler than a shaper of the regional order. It could obstruct its foes' designs through its alliances and proxies and help defuse crises that it often triggered or exacerbated. However, deprived of any real attributes of power, it could not impose its own regional architecture and security preferences on its neighbours in a meaningful way. This reality, though obscured by bombastic statements and defiant public diplomacy, squared badly with Assad's self-image as a pivotal Arab leader.

Over time, the relative power of Syria in its alliances with Iran and Hizbullah decreased. While Hafez al-Assad had a utilitarian appreciation of these allies, his son deepened the ideological and strategic commitment to this rejectionist front, seeking regional standing and legitimacy.[5] Ironically, Assad's dependence on the alliance with Iran and Hizbullah only grew as it brought Arab and Western policymakers to his door to convince him to abandon it. Whether Assad ever seriously considered doing so, as part of a grand bargain, is uncertain. Indeed, the assertion of Iranian power as a result of the US-induced collapse of Taliban rule in Afghanistan and of Saddam Hussein in Iraq, and the growing prominence of Iran's nuclear programme on the Middle East security agenda trapped Syria in a broader regional power play. Despite protestations to the contrary, Damascus had fewer cards to play: it could no longer guarantee the disarmament of Hizbullah or an automatic peace treaty with Lebanon (were one to be reached between Israel and Syria) as it could during the occupation of its tiny neighbour. Furthermore, with the rise of Iran, Israel's parameters for a peace deal had changed: an agreement would hinge on whether it would decisively curtail Iran's reach in the Levant.

Regional competition: between Turkey, Iran and the Gulf

The revolution catches the region by surprise
On the eve of the Syrian uprising, Assad had managed to cajole or outmanoeuvre most of his regional detractors. The resignation of Mubarak in Egypt, which the Syrian regime welcomed, and Saudi fear of further instability worked to his advantage. Indeed, the series of uprisings that shook the Arab world in 2011 at first cemented a regional consensus to prevent further revolutionary change, including in Syria.

The first sparks of the Syrian uprising in February 2011 were quickly extinguished and failed to attract the attention of Arab media, elites and publics, who were preoccupied with revolutions in Egypt and Libya and massive demonstrations in Yemen and Bahrain. An important reason for this lack of interest was a broadly shared assessment that the Assad regime's resilience in the face of previous domestic and foreign challenges made it uniquely prepared to face any such contingency and chances of an uprising less likely.

By the time the uprising witnessed its second, more durable tremor in Deraa in March 2011, other layers of complexity had been added. Averse to more upheaval, the Gulf monarchies proved anxious to contain the revolutionary tide, which had began to impinge on their interests. The demise of Hosni Mubarak, a long-standing and reliable ally, the sense that the US had proven naïve and incompetent in managing the Egyptian revolution and concern about the rise of the MB coloured the thinking of Gulf decision-makers. Assad secured temporary goodwill with Gulf officials by refraining from criticising their Bahrain intervention in support of the Al-Khalifah monarchy in March 2011. This was rewarded by the decision to omit the Syrian crisis from the Arab League agenda and benign media coverage in early months. Over the spring and summer, the Bahraini and Emirati foreign ministers visited Damascus with messages of thanks while Saudi King Abdullah offered mild public support to Assad.[6]

Turkey and the Gulf states engage Assad, then harden their position
Early on, Turkey and Qatar sought to capitalise on their strong ties with Assad to arrange a political soft-landing. As Assad's closest allies, they surmised they had unique leverage and a special responsibility. Moreover, a successful political settlement would have resonated throughout the region, adding to their influence and standing.

Accordingly, they pushed for a political settlement that would bring in new figures to the government without upsetting the foundations of the regime. They pressed Assad to grant minor political concessions such as lifting restrictions on Islamist movements (for instance, revoking the law that made membership in the MB a capital crime) and enlarging his cabinet to include Islamist and other opposition figures.[7] Gulf officials also pondered whether the budding political challenge to Assad could create an opportunity to sway Assad away from Iran by offering him Gulf capital, religious legitimacy and regional protection from international pressure. Assad rebuffed such ideas on the grounds that the political reforms he outlined in speeches in late March and April would suffice to placate domestic demands.

Turkey and several Arab states initially opposed US and EU sanctions on Syria, arguing that engagement would convince Assad to adopt a softer approach to domestic discontent. Repeated contacts between Assad and the Turkish and Qatari leaders yielded no result, however, except for significant political frustration and personal embarrassment. Frenetic Turkish diplomacy, including a six-hour meeting between Assad and Davutoglu in August 2011, failed to convince the former to suspend military operations in Hama and other areas and commit to a serious political dialogue.

Relations soured quickly as Assad saw the Qatari and Turkish mediation attempts as aimed at undermining his rule. Doha and Ankara had hosted initial meetings of the nascent Syrian opposition, hoping to build ties that could be used in a negotiation with Assad, but the Syrian media portrayed this as evidence that the country was the victim of an Islamist conspiracy, with Qatar and Turkey as lead schemers. Qatar had particularly good relations with the MB, and *al-Jazeera* carried forceful denunciations of Assad by Sheikh Youssef al-Qaradawi, an influential preacher affiliated with the MB. Moreover, the ties of Turkey's ruling party to the MB validated the notion of a broad collusion in Syrian eyes. In the Syrian state media, Erdogan was accused of using his friendship with Assad to further his own duplicitous Islamist and neo-Ottoman designs on the region.[8]

Gulf states seized this opportunity to register their discontent with Syria by thwarting its bid to win a seat traditionally reserved for an Arab state at the UN Human Rights Council (HRC) in the late spring. Arab states, which had previously abstained from UN HRC votes on Syria, began to introduce and support statements condemning the repression. The mounting acrimony peaked with the regime-backed storming of the Qatari embassy in Damascus in July 2011, followed by Qatar's decision to withdraw its diplomatic representation and freeze its projects in Syria.

The Gulf position hardened as regime repression garnered media attention and violence increased, especially during the holy month of Ramadan. The sense of religious outrage was amplified by footage of abuses coming from Syria, and a sectarian reading of the uprising by Gulf-based clerics with media access contributed to this shift in attitude. In Riyadh, an unprecedented demonstration took place outside the Syrian embassy, while in Kuwait and Bahrain Salafi and MB-inclined parliamentarians denounced the Assad regime's Alawite character and alliance with Iran, and demanded a break in relations. This culminated in a formal break of diplomatic relations in early August 2011, when Saudi Arabia, Kuwait and Bahrain recalled their ambassadors.

The rhetorical escalation against Assad was unmistakable and unprecedented, even by the standards of the acrimonious history of Syrian-Gulf relations. The first salvo came from the Saudi monarch in early August 2011: 'What is happening in Syria is not acceptable for Saudi Arabia ... Syria should think wisely before it's too late and issue and enact reforms that are not merely promises but actual reforms. Either it chooses wisdom on its own or it will be pulled down into the depths of turmoil and loss.'[9] Turkey was similarly outspoken in September of the same year, as Erdogan bluntly warned Assad that: 'Those who repress their own people in Syria will not survive. The time of autocracies is over. Totalitarian regimes are disappearing. The rule of the people is coming.'[10]

In private, Gulf officials confided that their ultimate objective was the ouster of Assad, but, at first, refrained from calling for this publicly and appeared reluctant to enter a head-on struggle with the Syrian regime. There was no appetite for a repeat of the Libya intervention given the magnitude and risk of such a venture, and the hesitancy of Western countries. The Gulf continued to support Arab League and UN diplomacy and, as late as September 2011, the Qatari Foreign Minister Hamad bin Jassem al-Thani articulated Gulf objectives in relatively cautious terms: 'The army must withdraw from inside the cities so that we can start talking about a dialogue between the people and the government ... There are those who cast doubt on some of the intentions [of the Arab League] ... but everyone supports Syria and its stability.'[11]

However, there was an awareness that the costs of weathering a civil war in Syria, and managing its regional spillover, would be considerable. The assessment that Syria would inevitably become a battlefield that would draw in external actors, including Iran, and would profoundly shape regional dynamics made involvement a geopolitical necessity for Gulf states and Turkey. The strategy that took shape in the final months of 2011 to confront the Assad regime had several prongs: close Turkish-Gulf diplomatic coordination; reliance on the Arab League as a legitimising and operational instrument; inscription of Assad's ouster within a transitional, UN-approved framework; seeking political and material backing of Western states, including at the UNSC; and overt and covert support for the Syrian opposition.

Turkey takes risks

For Turkey, the opportunity to protect its credibility, assert regional leadership and redress what the Turkish leadership saw as duplicity and personal affront by Assad came with considerable danger. By declaring Assad's ouster as his objective, Erdogan overturned his much-touted 'good neighbour'[12] policy and set an unprecedented and controversial test for Turkish power.

The unfolding conflict in Syria had significant repercussions for Turkish interests. Syria's civil war threatened its territorial integrity, which potentially had momentous implications for its own disenfranchised Kurdish community. Turkey was particularly exposed to the spillover of the crisis, such as the large influx of refugees and cross-border firefights; the economic well-being and stability of its heterogeneous southern regions could be affected too. Moreover, the collapse of the Syrian state would inevitably draw Ankara's regional rivals (Iran, Iraq and the Gulf states) into the Syrian arena, where it lacked natural allies.

From Ankara's perspective, ensuring that Syria did not transform into a source of threat and destabilisation required active engagement. At first, it seemed that Erdogan's determination benefitted Turkey's regional standing and shaped US, European and Arab approaches to Syria. These countries sought a regionally driven multilateral solution; in particular, Washington expected that regional leadership would adequately make up for its own reluctance for greater involvement.

As a front-line state, Turkey was expected to counsel and mentor the Syrian opposition, most notably the SNC, whose formation it had encouraged. This proved a fraught and damaging venture. Ankara maintained particularly good relations with the Syrian MB, whose influence within the SNC grew considerably, which led to accusations of Turkish (and Qatari) bias towards the MB. Conversely, opposition leaders felt, at first, buoyed by Erdogan's verbal belligerence but later betrayed by

Turkish operational indecision. Syrian Kurdish activists also blamed Turkey for the Arab-dominated opposition's lack of responsiveness to their demands on political decentralisation and citizenship. Ultimately, the infighting and ineffectiveness of the main Syrian opposition groups reflected badly on Turkey's ability to shepherd a credible and broad-based alternative to Assad rule.

Turkey also played a reluctant role as a de facto overseer of the armed opposition. Disparate rebel groups under the umbrella of the FSA had based themselves on its soil and the Turkish border became a prime conduit for arms smuggling, especially as rebels seized border zones and crossing points. Turkish self-interest dictated careful monitoring of these groups and activities, and calculated that cultivating them would also translate into leverage in the coming realignment of forces inside Syria. However, Ankara proved uncomfortable with and overwhelmed by the responsibility of coordinating material assistance to the rebels and reconciling the positions of the Gulf states and its Western allies over the level and quality of this assistance. A good example was the debate over the provision of advanced anti-aircraft weaponry. The Gulf states argued that such deliveries were necessary to combat Assad's air power in the absence of an internationally enforced no-fly zone, but the US was adamantly opposed to this over fears that such weapons would fall into the hands of jihadi groups. For its part, Turkey adopted a similar position, but out of concern that the weaponry could reach Kurdish militants inside Turkey.

Indeed, a primary driver of Turkish policy was the perceived impact of the Syrian crisis on Kurdish political and military behaviour. For Turkey, the danger resided in the emboldening of its own Kurdish separatists, the use of Syrian territory by the PKK to mount attacks, Assad's manipulation of his Kurdish allies and, in the medium term, the erosion of Syria's territorial integrity. Ironically, the very concern about these dangers prompted renewed attention in Ankara on Turkey's own Kurdish problem. By early 2013, the contours of a political process involving the PKK had emerged, with PKK leader Abdullah Ocalan announcing an indefinite ceasefire in March.

The Syrian Kurdish political spectrum appeared divided between the moderate KNC and the more radical PYD, a Syrian affiliate of the PKK, and Ankara credited the military gains of the PYD to a tacit understanding with the Assad regime. (Damascus withdrew from Kurdish territories in 2012, creating a security vacuum aimed in part to keep Turkey in check.) This left Ankara with limited options: direct intervention against the PYD would be militarily complex, would require incursions into Syrian territory and be framed as Ottoman imperialism and would unify Kurdish factions. Ankara's ties to the MB complicated any rapprochement with non-Islamist Syrian opposition factions. The KNC distrusted Islamist groups and blamed Ankara for the SNC's uncompromising stance on its demands. Ankara has, however, been able to leverage its rapidly improving relations with Iraq's KRG to influence Syria's Kurds and contain their ambitions.

By confronting Assad, Erdogan also exacerbated an already delicate relationship with neighbouring Iraq. Iraqi Prime Minister Nuri al-Maliki suspected Ankara of supporting his political adversaries to check his power and prevent the emergence of a strong, centralised Iraq. Accusations in Baghdad were rife that Turkish policy had taken a sectarian turn over Syria. In particular, Maliki resented Ankara's closeness to the KRG, with which he sparred over Kirkuk and oil policy, and its support for Sunni officials ostracised by Baghdad, including former Vice-President Tariq al-Hashimi, who found refuge on Turkish soil.

With Tehran, however, Ankara demonstrated greater caution, due to the significant economic and energy exchanges between the two countries that created complex interdependence, as well as Turkey's mediation role in Iran's controversial nuclear programme. As a result, Erdogan engaged in delicate diplomacy, urging Iran to abandon Assad while involving it in diplomatic efforts to end the conflict.

As Assad demonstrated greater resilience than expected, Turkey's inherent limitations were exposed. Critics claimed that Turkish policy had been driven by Erdogan's impulses rather than strategic prudence and that his early assessments had misjudged Assad's strength, overstated the appeal of the opposition and created false expectations about Turkey's ability to help it. In fact, despite a decade of high-level engagement, Turkish knowledge of Syrian society was paltry; commercial exchanges had not translated into societal ties and the foreign ministry and intelligence services lacked Arabic speakers with field experience and local contacts. Turkey also carried a heavy historical burden: suspicions that it was motivated by a neo-Ottoman, Islamist agenda ran deep in the Arab world, fuelling skepticism about Erdogan's ultimate intentions.

Ankara has turned to its Western allies for backing when its own shortcomings were magnified by events. Its lack of retaliatory options was exposed after a series of small yet embarrassing firefights. In the summer of 2012, the Syrian air defence downed a Turkish jet and Syrian mortars landed on Turkish soil. As a result, Ankara called for a tougher Western stance, including the imposition of a no-fly zone, and argued for greater US involvement in streamlining assistance to Syrian rebels. Ankara also floated the idea of creating a safe zone inside Syria to contain the escalating refugee crisis. The help Ankara got fell short of its expectations: it was of a defensive and limited nature, with the deployment in early 2013 of anti-missile *Patriot* batteries by NATO Allies. As Erdogan came to better appreciate his own constraints and the enduring nature of Western caution, Turkey started de-escalating its rhetoric and accommodating ideas for diplomacy, such as the stillborn regional Quartet that grouped it with Iran, Egypt and Saudi Arabia and engaged in talks with Russia.

Domestically, Erdogan faced considerable disapproval of his Syria policy, which compounded other criticisms of his tenure. Secular parties, including the leading opposition faction the Republican People's Party, accused him of pan-Islamist ambitions and adventurism, while many in the Alevi minority, which share a spiritual affinity with the Alawites, displayed similar misgivings. The conflict also affected the southern province of Hatay, where most Syrian refugees and rebels sought shelter, and which is home to a large community of Alawites of Arab origin sympathetic towards Assad. Finally, Erdogan's aggressive Syria policy further exacerbated relations with the Turkish military, whose influence the former had curtailed through constitutional, political and judicial moves.

By misjudging the costs of the struggle, Ankara exposed itself to domestic and international criticism. Erdogan's detractors maintained that he escalated too quickly and too hard, eschewing opportunities for diplomatic manoeuvring and endangering important relationships, and that his very objective to unseat Assad was as problematic as his failed strategy to do so. Western allies amplified the appearance of Turkish isolation and impotence by rejecting repeated Turkish demands for stronger action.

Nonetheless, Turkey remains essential to the dynamics of the conflict and Syria's future. Its role in any negotiated solution, transition and reconstruction initiative will be central. Still, many Syrians are worried about Turkey's ambitions and the extent to which it would be a fair partner. This concern centres on whether it would sacrifice its alliances with Islamist factions, for the benefit of a more inclusive political settlement, and whether it would be able to articulate a policy that did not alienate important segments of Syrian society, especially the Kurds.

The Gulf states back the opposition but differ over strategy

The position of the Gulf states hinged on the assessment that the ethno-confessional breakdown, sectarian loyalties and weak states in the Levant had created a more malleable environment. The prospect of regime change in Syria held much promise, as the Gulf monarchies were profoundly inimical to the Assad regime: a Ba'athist, Alawite-dominated, secular, pseudo-republican government that ran a socialist economy, was aligned with Iran and Hizbullah and manipulated the Palestinian cause.

The strategic rationale for overthrowing Assad was compelling: it would reverse Iran's reach in the Levant; contribute to the weakening of Hizbullah in Lebanon; make up for the perceived loss of Iraq and perhaps embolden Sunni opposition to the Shia-dominated central government in Baghdad; punish Assad for his alliances and previous behaviour; recover the Palestinian card from the grip of the rejectionist camp; and bring to power an allied, possibly compliant Sunni leadership. Importantly, they saw the make-up of Syria, where Sunni Arabs clearly dominated, as working to their advantage.

These calculations needed, however, to be measured against the significant risks and costs of induced-regime change. The effort to unseat Assad would demand significant resources and strategic patience. Firstly, intervention in Syria, whether covert or overt, would antagonise both Iran and Iraq, risking an escalation with direct impact on Persian Gulf security. Secondly, for reasons of geography and capabilities, the Gulf states alone could not effect decisive change in Syria and thus depended on Turkish and Western commitment and involvement. Thirdly, the Gulf states exposed their own inconsistency regarding political change: as autocracies repressing their own minorities and dissenters, their claim to promote democracy in Syria came across as hollow and hypocritical. Sectarian agitation and rhetoric in the Gulf about a 'Shia crescent'[13] – rife since the empowerment of

Shia factions in Iraq – couched the struggle over Syria in distinctively communal terms. Finally, many possible outcomes could adversely affect Gulf interests and stability, including the destabilisation of Jordan, the spread of the violence into Lebanon, the rise of the MB and renewed jihadi activism.

As they deepened their engagement in Syria, the Gulf states displayed considerable deficiencies: a weak understanding of the complex Syrian terrain; an overreliance on Islamist, tribal and regime contacts that did not reflect the diversity of Syrian society; little expertise at conducting complex intelligence operations abroad; and intense competition and lack of coordination over strategy and patronage of Syrian opposition groups. As a result, they were forced to outsource much of their outreach to the armed groups to Lebanese, Turkish, Iraqi and Jordanian middlemen.

Saudi Arabia and Qatar emerged as prime backers of the Syrian opposition. They mobilised funding, media power (respectively *al-Arabiya* and *al-Jazeera*, but also more sectarian channels such as *Wesal*), religious clout (Saudi Arabia sees itself as the champion of Sunni Islam) and political muscle in the service of the Syrian rebel cause. Gulf-based clerics contributed to the demonisation of the Assad regime and in stirring up sectarian sentiments. They also allowed the Syrian diaspora to organise and fundraise, discreetly, on their soil, although the UAE forbade such activities for fear that political mobilisation would inspire its own dissidents.

Nevertheless, concern over blowback informed Gulf, and in particular Saudi, policy.[14] Governments were keen to prevent a repetition of the instability and radicalisation afflicted on their societies by jihadi fighters returning from Afghanistan, Bosnia and Iraq. Consequently, a senior Saudi cleric issued a *fatwa* forbidding local men from joining the jihad in Syria and clerics were urged by the Saudi authorities to refrain from fundraising for Syrian rebel groups.[15] This met with mixed results: there was evidence of Saudi and Gulf fighters present in Syria, including in lists of captured foreign fighters communicated by the Syrian government to the UN in late 2012.[16]

The Gulf states also advocated greater backing for the Syrian opposition, including directly arming them. To bypass Western reluctance, in April 2012, Saudi Arabia, Qatar and the UAE announced a US$100m fund to distribute salaries to rebel fighters affiliated to the FSA (though it remains unclear whether this mechanism was put into practise). The provision of weaponry to the rebels by the Gulf states became a matter of controversy, and they refrained from sending sophisticated weapon systems, due to Western (and Turkish) opposition.[17] Instead, they delivered small and light weaponry, much of which came from Libyan arsenals,[18] and, later, Riyadh and Doha set up an operations centre in Turkey charged with identifying and sponsoring suitable rebel units.[19] They also leaned on Jordan, reluctant at first to be used to support the Syrian rebellion, to allow opposition fighters to organise from its soil.[20]

Quickly, however, differences emerged between Saudi Arabia, Qatar and the UAE over their interests, strategy and patronage. The three countries cultivated competing constituencies and interlocutors inside Syria, and embraced differing visions for the country's future. Saudi Arabia relied on: strong ties with key trans-regional tribal groups with a presence in both Syria and the Kingdom; Islamist networks and the many Syrians who had embraced Salafism as expatriates in the Gulf; and defected regime figures, from both pre- and post-2011, such as Rifaat al-Assad, Abdel Halim Khaddam and Manaf Tlass. For its part, Qatar maintained an alliance with the Syrian MB, along with a variety of Islamist groups, but this conflicted with the UAE's own pronounced antagonism towards the MB. As a result, the UAE distanced itself from the MB-dominated SNC and actively contributed to the formation of the broader NC, in which the MB's power was, theoretically, diluted.

By late 2012, it became clear that the Gulf states had underestimated the strength of the Assad regime and the costs associated
with dislodging it, as the rapid transformation of the uprising
into a sectarian civil war proved beyond their capacity to manage.
They remained frustrated about Western policy, which was torn
between the fading hope of a diplomatic solution and the reality
of a worsening civil war. Their clumsy attempts to arm various
opposition groups had not translated into actual leverage, but
rather given birth to competing factions and escalating demands
for funding and weaponry. Private Gulf funding poured into
radical Islamist factions, at the expense of mainstream units, and
now threatens the fabric of Syrian society. Ominously, the Gulf
states had invested little in preparing the transition from Assad
rule and planning for the institutional and physical reconstruction of Syria.

Iran: stuck with Assad

No country stands to lose more from, or was less prepared
for, the sustained challenge to Assad rule than Iran, Syria's
long-standing ally. Their three-decade-old relationship had
periodically been troubled as their interests, at times, diverged.
Yet it had proven to be a political and strategic partnership that
was resilient and mutually beneficial. It was based on common
threat perceptions and a joint opposition to a regional order
dominated by the US, Israel and their Arab allies, but also on
a mutual recognition that their alliance was a force-multiplier.
Since Bashar al-Assad came to power, it had gained even greater
importance for both countries strategically, as well as developing a thicker ideological veneer. The increasing assertiveness
of hardline factions in Tehran, Iran's growing regional clout and
the rise of Hizbullah as its third pillar shifted the power within
the alliance towards Iran.

Despite this, Iran had, at first, welcomed the Arab uprisings
as they had uprooted Western-aligned autocrats and under-

mined the Gulf states' strategic interests. The Iranian Supreme Leader Ayatollah Ali Khamenei hailed them as an 'Islamic awakening'[21] inspired in large part by Iran's own Islamic revolution. Unsurprisingly, Iran dismissed the initial Syrian revolutionary tremors, which did not fit this ideological and strategic prism, as the work of criminal gangs and marginal elements of Syrian society, in effect espousing the narrative propagated by Assad. This initial reaction betrayed a lack of knowledge of Syrian society, demonstrating that the strong strategic and security bonds had not translated into societal interactions able to inform Iranian thinking.

However, the prominent role of the MB and other Islamist factions, ostensibly sympathetic to the values of the Islamic Republic, the potency of the challenge faced by Assad and Iran's steep drop in popularity and standing throughout the Arab world, as a result of its support for Assad, prompted new debate in Tehran. Clumsy efforts were made to reach out to Syrian opposition factions, especially Islamist ones and those that did not call for Assad's ouster. Tehran counselled dialogue with the regime, which it, meanwhile, feebly encouraged to adopt a less repressive approach to dissent. These attempts proved largely futile as, by this point, the growing sectarian undertones of the struggle had amplified the perception of Iran as a Shia expansionist power, with much of the Syrian opposition seeing Iran as firmly on Assad's side, out of Alawite-Shia solidarity, and complicit in its ruthless repression. While Syrian protesters routinely vilified Iran, regime loyalists praised its pro-Assad commitment.

Ultimately, regardless of the intensity of the debate in Tehran over the wisdom, merits and cost of shoring up Assad, strategic and contingency imperatives prevailed over hedging considerations. These included helping him survive the uprising, securing supply lines to Hizbullah, countering the suspected Gulf involvement in Syria but also developing a presence to be used should the regime collapse. The assessment that instability in Syria would inevitably draw in other foreign powers required early and sustained involvement to secure Iran's own interests.

Assad's fall would greatly complicate Iran's position in the Middle East. The prospect, however remote, of Syria being governed by a government aligned with its regional rivals would amount to a strategic and symbolic setback for Tehran. As its sole and reliable Arab partner, Syria had served to attenuate accusations that the Islamic Republic harboured a Persian and Shia hegemonic agenda at odds with Arab and Sunni interests. It facilitated relations with rejectionist Palestinian factions – including Hamas before it distanced itself from Damascus. This provided legitimacy to Iran's foreign policy, which prospered on championing Arab and Muslim causes seemingly abandoned by Arab governments accused of servility to the West. More importantly, Syria provides a valuable logistical route into Lebanon and strategic depth to Hizbullah, the Shia militant group that serves as an instrument of deterrence and retaliation against Israel and the US. All these gains would likely be nullified by a new government dominated by Sunni Islamists or aligned with the Gulf states and Turkey.

Within months of the start of the uprising, Tehran started mobilising assets to support its Syrian ally. A visit by General Qassem Suleimani, the commander of the Iranian Revolutionary Guards Corps' elite Quds Force, to Damascus in January 2012 appeared to have upped and sealed that commitment. Drawing on its own experience in quelling political dissent and domestic insurgencies, Iran's support included: expertise in Internet and communications monitoring; help in circumventing oil and other sanctions imposed by the US, the EU and the Arab League; deliveries of ammunition and weaponry; intelligence-sharing; counter-insurgency advice; and personnel from the Quds and Bassij forces. Furthermore, after unsubstantiated sightings of Iranian security personnel deployed alongside regime forces, in August 2012 Syrian rebels captured 48 Iranian men. Initially portrayed by Tehran as innocent pilgrims and later as retired military personnel, they were released in a prisoner swap with rebel forces through indirect Turkish channels in early 2013, without official Iranian recognition of their belonging to its security forces.[22] This suggested an Iranian military commitment considerably greater than had been thought.

Iran's support for Assad took on a political dimension as well. Through official statements, media propaganda and in multilateral forums, Tehran sought to reinforce Assad's portrayal of the uprising as part of a wider, Western-backed conspiracy aimed at the *jabhat al-mumana'a*, or rejectionist front. In a religious sermon in October 2012, Khamenei described Syria's unfolding conflict as 'a crime initiated by the United States and the Zionist regime, Israel'.[23] The Non-Aligned Movement summit, held in Tehran in August 2012, also gave the Iranians a platform to voice their support for Assad, and Ali Akbar Velayati, a top adviser to Khamenei, described Assad's fate as a 'red line' to Iran's own security.[24]

The conflict in Syria has had a knock-on effect on Iran's other regional alliances, which it has, in some cases, been able to leverage to back Assad. For example, Tehran and Hizbullah's overlapping interests in Syria led to their joint intervention in the conflict. Another direct effect of the Syrian crisis has been a greater, interest-based alignment between Iran and Iraq, allowing Iran to supply Assad with weaponry and financial assistance through Iraq.

However, the uprising has further complicated relations between Iran and Turkey, which had improved through growing energy and commercial ties, Turkey's good-neighbourhood policy and Erdogan's interest in preventing a showdown between Iran and its Western allies. Despite this, geopolitical rivalry had remained strong, as the inroads Turkey had made into the Arab world were a threat to Iran's regional position: Erdogan's bombastic support for the Palestinians and growing profile in the Israeli-Arab arena eroded Iran's appeal to Arabs. Relations also soured over Turkey's decision in September 2011 to host an early-warning radar system on its soil, which was part of a NATO missile-defence architecture ostensibly aimed at Iran.

Following the uprising, relations cooled further as Ankara and Tehran articulated fundamentally different objectives and clashing strategies. Iran sought to check Turkish assertiveness and its perceived power play in the Levant. Turkey's leading role in the diplomatic effort to unseat Assad and its sponsorship of the Syrian opposition irritated Iran, which saw Sunni solidarity and geopolitical manoeuvring to be Erdogan's motivation. Tensions between the two countries peaked with Turkish accusations of Iranian support of Kurdish separatist militants emboldened by events in Syria. In November 2012, Turkish Interior Minister Idris Naim Sahin told Turkish media: 'We are quite aware of Iran's support for the PKK ... We know that PKK members that are wounded during clashes against the Turkish army are treated in Iranian hospitals.'[25] Despite rising tensions, both recognised that the stakes were high (owing to their economic and energy interdependence) and tempered escalatory instincts. For example, Ankara gave muted public responses to reports that Iran was sending weaponry to Syria via Turkey, even as it loudly protested Russian arms deliveries crossing its airspace.[26]

Iran's treatment of the Syrian crisis can be seen as opportunistic as well, approaching it as a way to break its own isolation and ensure it would be part of any negotiated settlement, however unlikely that may be. Engaging Iran diplomatically and leveraging its influence over Assad were seen by Kofi Annan (the first Joint Special Envoy of the UN and Arab League) and his successor Lakhdar Brahimi as essential elements for a negotiated resolution and a smooth transition of power. Of course, many in the West and the Arab world worried that this would give Tehran undue recognition and turn Syria into another arena for regional competition. The formation of a regional quartet gave rise to another opportunity for Iranian engagement. In an attempt to define a new foreign policy less dependent on the US, Egypt's new president, Muhammad Morsi, called on Turkey, Saudi Arabia and Iran to join a Syria contact group, which Tehran enthusiastically did, keen as it was to prove its regional relevance. The initiative, despite receiving lip service at first, stagnated as Riyadh and Ankara fundamentally differed with Tehran over the wisdom and mechanics of a negotiated transition.

The dire consequences of the fall of Assad for Iran need to be balanced by its proven ability to adapt and navigate contentious politics and fault lines in weak states. In Lebanon, Iraq and Afghanistan, Iran has succeeded in nurturing allies and proxies and in developing influence over their domestic and foreign policies. Its growing presence in Syria, primarily through the training of pro-regime militias, may well be intended to cultivate and exploit relationships regardless of the fate of the Assad regime. This suggests Iran has engaged in contingency planning, so that its interests could still be adequately served if Syria fragments and descends into a protracted civil war.

Iraq: the spectre of sectarian war reappears

The transformation of the Syrian revolution into a civil war threatened to reignite sectarian passions inside Iraq just as Nuri al-Maliki, the Iraqi prime minister, has moved to consolidate his power and decisively contain the beleaguered opposition to his authority.

Between the fall of the regime of Saddam Hussein in 2003 and the Syrian revolution, relations between Baghdad and Damascus had been hostile. The Syrian government, which had vocally opposed the US occupation of Iraq, had supported the various resistance movements against US troops and the new power structure in Baghdad. Damascus harboured remnants of the Saddam regime and Ba'ath Party members. To build leverage in Iraq and bog down US troops, Syrian intelligence services facilitated and, at times, manipulated the activities of jihadi fighters, including al-Qaeda affiliates, primarily by allowing the use of Syria as prime entry point into Iraq and through the provision of logistical support.

By early 2011, Maliki had successfully reasserted the authority of the central government over much of Iraq, defeating both Sunni insurgents and Shia competitors with US help.[27] He had also obtained the complete withdrawal of the US military presence, leaving him in charge of the country's security and foreign policy. Higher oil prices gave him resources to placate domestic constituencies and rebuild the administrative and coercive capacity of the Iraqi state, especially the military. He moved to politically co-opt, defeat and isolate his Shia and Sunni rivals, while clashing politically with the KRG over oil policy, territorial issues such as Kirkuk and the reach of the state.

As fear over the trajectory of the Syrian uprising was balanced against deep enmity towards Assad, Iraq's central government found it difficult at first to calibrate its policy. Domestically, the Syrian uprising had the potential to galvanise Iraq's own dejected and increasingly marginalised Sunni community. A fractured Syria, with a government not in control of its territory and its porous borders, could reinvigorate and become a haven for Sunni groups opposed to perceived Shia rule, allowing for the rebirth of jihadi groups. A worrying development is the re-emergence of AQI, through JN in Syria. AQI has been significantly degraded militarily and its tactics and radicalism alienated large sections of the Sunni community, but the Syrian uprising has offered it an opening to recast itself and make use of its veteran fighters before reorienting its efforts onto Iraq. Renewed Kurdish assertiveness in Syria is a further concern for Maliki, as it could bolster Iraq's own Kurds against his attempts to centralise power. Syria's contagious collapse could lead to the spillover of Syrian Kurdish-Arab tensions – Sunni Arabs also resent Kurdish autonomy and their claim over the oil-rich city of Kirkuk. The possibility of clashes in Syria extending to northern Iraq and creating instability that would benefit the PKK has prompted greater KRG-Turkish cooperation.

Regionally, the competition over Syria directly affected Iraq. The Iraqi government remained ostracised by the Gulf states, the main supporters of the Syrian opposition. Gulf officials themselves framed their intervention in Syria as an attempt to repair the perceived loss of Iraq to Shia power and saw an opportunity to weaken Baghdad by grooming a Sunni government on its western border. Over the medium term, the possible rise of an antagonistic Sunni-dominated state in Syria could lead to the emergence of a regional and sectarian rival.

Iraq, at first, settled on a policy of uneasy neutrality, but, as the uprising gained a sectarian Sunni character, Maliki steered Iraqi policy towards support for Assad. This shift resulted from his assessment of the dire strategic and security risks to his own authority, as well as the calculation that, in doing so, he lost no constituency at home that didn't already oppose him. It also allowed him to tap into festering Shia resentment against Sunnis for the long and deadly civil war fought since 2003. Furthermore, Maliki's support offered political respite to Assad: he condemned any foreign intervention in Syria and called for a strictly Syrian resolution facilitated by regional mediation; and when Iraq hosted the annual meeting of the Arab League in 2012, Maliki rallied Arab states opposed to regime change in Damascus against the Gulf states.

At the time of writing, there is no evidence that Maliki has provided direct support for Assad, but there have been unsubstantiated allegations that Syria has used Iraqi financial institutions to circumvent sanctions. Iraqi authorities have also allowed the use of their territory for Iranian transfers of weaponry, and Hizbullah has trained Iraqi Shia fighters that later deployed in Syria to protect Shia sites.[28]

Controlling Iraq's restive Sunni provinces, of al-Anbar, Salaheddine and Nineveh, and its long and porous border with Syria have become a priority. Iraqi security forces were deployed to stem the flow of Sunni fighters and assistance going into Syria and they also attempted to take over the parts of the border controlled by the KRG, but Kurdish peshmergas resisted. This had a marginal impact, however, given the rough terrain and cross-border kinship (tribal links connect large groups in Syria, Iraq, Jordan and Saudi Arabia), and the Iraqi border has become a main conduit for weaponry to the Syrian rebellion and Iraqi Sunni fighters who have joined rebel ranks.

The increasingly sectarian character of the Syrian uprising couldn't but resonate within Iraq, where no significant reconciliation has occurred and where all levers of power have come to rest with Maliki and his allies at the expense of other groups, importantly the Sunni Arab minority. A Sunni-dominated Syria or the mere expulsion of Assad forces from the eastern parts of the country could offer strategic and military depth to an armed and political challenge to Maliki's authority in the western part of Iraq. Already, a Sunni protest movement has emerged in reaction to Maliki's crackdown on both Sunni and rival Shia politicians, including members of the rival al-Iraqiya faction and former Vice-President al-Hashimi. Saddam's deposed Vice-President Izzet Ibrahim Ad-Douri, who had found refuge in Syria, has also called on Ba'athist remnants in Iraq to mobilise against Maliki. It remains unlikely that the various Sunni groups could mount a campaign to reclaim power from Maliki, but a more plausible scenario would be a new and more localised insurgency in the western parts of the country aimed at pushing out government forces and establishing de facto autonomy. Such a rebellion would further complicate Maliki's position towards the Kurds by possibly providing the latter with new allies and another route into the Mediterranean.

Vulnerable states: Lebanon and Jordan

Lebanon: the risk of contagion

It is no surprise that the Syrian uprising has amplified Lebanon's own fault lines and further eroded the resilience of its already-battered state institutions. Its organic links to Syria and unique exposure to regional dynamics make it a particularly vulnerable state to the fallout of the Syrian crisis.

The Assad regime had always considered Lebanon to be part of its strategic orbit: the control of its smaller neighbour aimed to affirm Syrian power in the Levant and deny its internal and regional enemies a base. Lebanon's complex and permeable sectarian politics had allowed Damascus to dominate its domestic affairs and security policy since 1990. Overreach by Assad and changing regional politics, however, led to peaceful Lebanese mobilisation and international rejection of the Syrian military occupation, which ended in 2005. Syria remained an actor in Lebanese politics by projecting influence through its Lebanese proxies and allies, including Hizbullah, and backing the latter during the 2006 war with Israel.

This influence had survived the turmoil in the run-up to 2011, as Western engagement and the rapprochement with Saudi Arabia, that began in 2008, undermined the fragile anti-Syrian coalition known as March 14. In January 2011, this coalition crumbled, bringing down the government of Saad Hariri, which opened the way for a new cabinet dominated by the pro-Syrian March 8 faction and led by an Assad-friendly prime minister, Najib Mikati.

Ironically, just as Assad was consolidating his influence over Lebanon, his authority at home was being challenged by the revolution, which was welcomed by the March 14 camp. Having branded Assad the cause of Lebanon's instability, but watched him outmanoeuvre them politically, his weakening by Syrian forces ostensibly aligned with their own interests. For the rival March 8 camp, now in power, the revolution in Syria undermined a key patron, as well as the narrative of resistance to Western hegemony they promoted.

All mainstream factions recognised the significant risks that could be incurred by Syria's civil war, namely violent contagion spreading to Lebanon. There is wide acknowledgment that the costs of a renewed civil war would be massive and of a debilitating, pervasive and sectarian nature. Military gains, for any group, would have a marginal political return given the locked nature of Lebanese politics, where positions and privileges are distributed along confessional lines, and as no single community represents more than a third of the population. While the balance of power on the ground tilts towards the March 8 camp, given Hizbullah's military superiority, alone this coalition could neither govern the polarised country nor hold its frail institutions together, especially the Lebanese military. As a result, the main political factions have been eager to avoid a direct confrontation at home, instead adopting a wait-and-see approach while vocally (and at times materially) supporting their respective allies in Syria.

By mid-2011, a centrist view had emerged among top officials and politicians that Lebanon needed to be shielded from the tremors coming out of Syria. The responsibility of holding the country together fell to Lebanese President Michel Suleiman and Mikati. A Sunni politician from Tripoli, a hotbed of support for the Syrian revolution, Mikati found himself walking an increasingly precarious tightrope in his role as prime minister. As a result, the Lebanese government articulated an uneasy policy of neutrality, dubbed 'dissociation', which Mikati outlined as follows: 'Lebanon's cabinet will continue to disassociate itself from Syria's conflict in order to preserve internal stability and safeguard the country from the possible repercussions of the region's turmoil.'[29]

In practice, this policy meant that Lebanon, which served as a member of the UNSC until late 2011, abstained and dissociated itself from UN statements criticising the Syrian government, and followed a similar approach at the Arab League, opting out of Arab League sanctions on Syria adopted in November 2011. Dissociation received the much-needed acquiescence of key Western and Arab states, as there was consensus on the unique exposure of Lebanon, the structural weakness of the state, and the need to contain the regional spillover of the Syrian crisis.

The viability of dissociation, however, depended primarily on volatile domestic factors, plus the ability and willingness of each faction to control its followers. Highly charged debate over Syria threatened to ignite local violence and compound other internal disputes and it did not take long for the conflict to seep into Lebanon. The strong ties that bind Syrian and Lebanese societies, including trans-border familial, tribal and economic relations, ensured that Lebanese politics quickly, if imperfectly, mirrored the struggle in Syria.

Inevitably, the Syrian revolution energised Assad's Lebanese detractors, a broad section of society made up mainly of Sunnis, Christians and Druze. Enthusiasm from among the Sunni community, still afflicted by bitter memories of the Syrian occupation and seeking revenge, was unmistakable. The uprising also mobilised Assad's allies, a segment of comparable political and demographic weight comprising mostly Shia, Christians and, notably, the small Alawite community. The increasingly sectarian narrative attached to the Syrian crisis aggravated the already contentious struggle in Beirut, with Sunni-Shia competition over power and the Christian community divided. However, a sizeable segment of Lebanese society has remained non-aligned, worried about importing Syria's troubles.

This potential for locally driven violence was realised early. By June 2011, several Syrian Sunni villages along the Lebanese border were subject to regime violence; this forced thousands of refugees and dozens of fighters to seek sanctuary in Lebanon's northern region of Wadi Khaled. In later months, the Syrian-Lebanese border, from the north to the Bekaa region, became a conduit for weapons, fighters and humanitarian assistance into Syria. Strong cross-border ties, a history of smuggling and weak or complacent security measures facilitated this. The multi-confessional fabric of the Bekaa valley and of northern Lebanon made these areas particularly volatile, as the uneasy cohabitation in the former of large Sunni and Shia communities and in the latter of a small but staunchly pro-Assad Alawite community amid the Sunni majority combined with a history of communal violence to compound state neglect and poverty. Furthermore, accusations were rife that security personnel coordinated with pro-Assad forces in this region.[30]

In Tripoli, besieged Alawite militiamen repeatedly clashed with Sunni combatants belonging to myriad factions, while tensions between Sunnis and Shia also rose, leading to occasional firefights in Beirut and Saida. Across the country, and in the absence of a genuine political dialogue, local deals and the intervention of the Lebanese military – generally seen as the country's least politicised and least sectarian security force –succeeded, on the whole, in quelling the violence.

Lebanon has become increasingly entangled in the fighting as it has spilt across the border, and has, in many ways, become an integral part of the geography of the Syrian struggle. For the Assad regime, securing the Alawite heartland in Syria required clearing a corridor of Sunni villages located among Alawite, Shia and Christian ones between Homs and the Lebanese border. The town and vicinity of Qusayr, southwest of Homs and only ten kilometres from the Lebanese border, therefore witnessed intense fighting that drew in anti-Assad Lebanese fighters and pro-regime Hizbullah Shia militiamen deployed to defend their religious brethren.

This entanglement has taken other pernicious forms as well. For example, several Lebanese Shia individuals, wrongly accused of being Hizbullah militants, were kidnapped inside Syria in the summer of 2012. This provoked retaliatory kidnappings of Syrians in Lebanon by Shia clans. When the extent of Hizbullah's involvement in Syria was revealed, Syrian rebel commanders announced they would take the fight to Lebanon and punish the Shia militia, prompting fears about attacks inside Lebanon against Shia religious sites and Hizbullah assets. In November 2012, two dozen Lebanese Sunni combatants were killed in a regime ambush, after they had entered Syria to fight alongside the rebellion.

There have been political consequences of the polarisation over Syria. Disillusionment among the Sunni community after a perceived loss of political influence to Hizbullah in previous years had already weakened its traditional, mainstream leadership. The Syrian uprising injected new momentum into Lebanon's small but increasingly vocal Lebanese Salafi and MB factions. By appealing to communal fears and creating a sense of purpose, these relatively marginal groups managed to reenter the political scene. Pro-revolution politicians from the local branch of the MB, various Salafi groups and associates of the Hariri faction have taken an active part in sheltering Syrian defectors, running logistical networks, fundraising and recruiting Lebanese fighters.

The Syrian crisis has eroded the already-limited capacity of the Lebanese state. Areas along the badly demarcated border have witnessed continuous violence and shelling by Syrian forces targeting smugglers and rebel fighters operating there, causing destruction and death. The lack of a military or diplomatic response has exposed the inherent weaknesses and limitations of the Lebanese government. The toll was particularly heavy for the Lebanese economy: regional trade crossed through Syria, Lebanese banks had significant exposure there and instability drove tourists away and affected investment and consumption in 2011 and 2012.[31]

The mounting refugee crisis is another cause for concern for the fragile Lebanese polity. Over 200,000 Syrian refugees, mostly Sunni, had already entered Lebanon by early 2013, stirring up fears that a long conflict would lead to their permanent settlement and upset the country's already delicate demographic balance.[32] Wealthier Syrians also relocated to Lebanon without registering as refugees. The expectation of a major battle in Damascus, only 40km from the Lebanese border, presaged another massive influx.

As he fought for his survival, Assad saw Lebanon as a place to raise the stakes and make clear his ability to project power and punish. He relied on local allies to repress Syrian dissidents, and sympathetic Lebanese security personnel kidnapped and handed over several Syrian activists. In August 2012, a prominent Lebanese ally of the Syrian regime, Michel Samaha, was arrested and charged with plotting major bombings at the behest of Assad and his top intelligence adviser, General Ali Mamlouk. In October 2012, Wissam al-Hassan, a senior security official responsible for the Samaha arrest who also secretly liaised with Syrian rebels, was killed in a massive car bombing in Beirut.

Hizbullah's dilemma

The weakening of the Assad regime poses a particular challenge for its main Lebanese ally, the Shia militant group Hizbullah. Strategic interests and loyalty for past sponsorship dictated steadfast cooperation: Syria, its ideological and strategic ally, provided a logistical hub and strategic depth. However, the costs of defending Assad have required subtle manoeuvring to manage the erosion of its standing and credibility in Lebanon, Syria and the broader Arab world. Hizbullah's activities in support of Assad have had to be calibrated to minimise Sunni rancour and a regional backlash.

This has forced Hizbullah into a difficult position. Its secretary-general, Hassan Nasrallah, has repeatedly stressed his support for the Assad regime and embraced its narrative while urging negotiations with the 'loyal opposition' that had no foreign backing and accepted dialogue with the regime. Domestically, the Shia guerrilla movement has maintained its support for the Lebanese government, recognising that the current political configuration was the best it could hope for and that political instability would further erode its standing. It has relied on the Lebanese military and intelligence agencies to maintain domestic order, fearing that its weaker Sunni rivals, angry and emboldened by the Syrian revolution, would mount a direct challenge. Hizbullah's desire to avoid a security showdown in Lebanon conflicts with Assad's apparent desire to export the conflict next door, as suggested by the thwarted Samaha plot and the al-Hassan assassination.

At the same time, Hizbullah has deepened its military involvement in Syria, in support of the regime,[33] by: securing old supply lines and developing new ones; providing manpower and expertise; preparing contingency plans in case of Assad's fall; countering Lebanese support for the Syrian rebels; and ensuring that its Lebanese foes do not manipulate the crisis to their advantage. By mid-2012, the extent of Hizbullah's involvement in Syria became clear, primarily because of the public burials of several fighters killed 'while performing their jihadi duties'.[34] In November 2012, reports surfaced that Hizbullah units were deployed around sensitive Syrian facilities, including those housing chemical weapons, and Hizbullah fighters have reportedly been training and operating with Syrian forces along the border, around Homs and south of Damascus.[35]

Jordan: caught between impossible choices
The Syrian uprising and its regional ramifications have magnified concerns about the precarious stability of the Hashemite

kingdom. Dense societal relations connect them and the two countries belong to the same strategic landscape. For resource-poor Jordan, still affected by Iraq's long civil war, the prospect of facing another similar, or more protracted, conflict and the fragmentation of the Syrian state would have far-reaching implications.

At the outset of the Syrian revolution, the Hashemite monarchy was fending off its own, though significantly milder, popular challenge over similar grievances. The political and economic record of King Abdullah of Jordan came under unprecedented criticism from diverse segments of Jordanian society. Through promises of political reform, government reshuffles, increased state spending and also state repression, the monarchy managed to placate and constrain demands. Jordan's exposure is underlined by physical proximity: Deraa, the birthplace of the Syrian uprising, is located on the Houran plateau, which extends into Jordan.

Jordan appeared at first ambivalent about regime change in Syria. Despite decades of animosity between the two regimes, change in Damascus was not necessarily seen to be in Amman's interest. Jordan faced similar Islamist threats, and the primary concern was that unrest in Syria could destabilise the monarchy and would inspire Jordan's own opposition. In particular, Jordan's own MB movement, known as the Islamic Action Front, would feel invigorated by their Syrian counterparts' rise, and other groups would be emboldened by the struggle and successes of Islamists across the border.

As the repression and the violence hit Deraa's and Damascus' peripheral districts, Syrian refugees sought shelter in Jordan, and the Jordanian government has struggled to cope with this refugee crisis. As of late 2012, over 100,000 refugees lived in camps but many more have not registered,[36] as their familial and tribal ties to Jordan have provided them with shelter and food outside official channels. Furthermore, Jordan's porous border and proximity to major Syrian centres have made it a conduit for weapons and fighters into Syria, but also a preferred destination for military and political defectors, such as Riyad Hijab. Military defectors used Jordanian territory to regroup, organise and prepare operations inside Syria, and the Deraa MC based itself in the border area. Small skirmishes have also taken place between Syrian and Jordanian border guards, prompting Jordan to deploy troops along its border.

By late 2012, it became increasingly evident that Jordan was implicated in the attempts to bolster the Syrian political and armed opposition. This shift was prompted by the intensification of the fighting in southern Syria, the desire of Saudi Arabia to develop alternative supply routes to non-MB-affiliated rebel groups and subtle changes in US policy. Better quality weaponry of Croatian origin acquired by Saudi intermediaries was delivered through Jordanian facilitation to select Syrian rebel groups and accounted for a series of rebel victories.

The broader regional context has had an impact on Jordan's evolving position on Syria. From early 2012, the Gulf states showed readiness to intervene in Syria through funding and arming rebel groups, but lacked the required channels and expertise. Jordan was uniquely positioned for that purpose, as its intelligence service, acknowledged as one of the best in the region, had unique access into Syria. Increasingly a client-state of the Gulf sheikhdoms, Jordan had grown dependent on crucial Gulf investment and financial assistance. In exchange for facilitating intelligence and support operations, Amman could expect crucial funding at a difficult time for the monarchy. Importantly, the Gulf states could provide much-needed political cover for the monarchy, internationally but also at home, and the influence of Qatar, Saudi Arabia and Turkey over the MB could help placate and contain Jordan's own political dissent.

The West's attention has also influenced Jordan. The monarchy's professed Western orientation and its peace treaty with Israel made Western governments particularly vested in Jordan's stability, which is seen as an essential line of defence for Israel. Gradual Western moves towards supporting the Syrian opposition and contingency-planning for the collapse of the Assad regime have both relied on Jordanian facilitation. The concern over Assad's chemical and missile arsenals led the US to deploy a task force of military personnel in Jordan to prepare for the fallout of these possible scenarios. Jordanian air defences have also been bolstered, and Jordanian territory will prove indispensable to support a no-fly zone or create a buffer zone.

For Jordan, however, involvement in Syria comes with major risks. The Assad regime could well target and punish the monarchy through local Jordanian proxies. The refugee crisis could spiral out of control, especially if Damascus experiences heavy fighting, sectarian cleansing occurs or chemical weapons are used. Blowback is also a serious concern, as many Jordanian jihadi fighters, especially from the town of Zarqa, have joined the armed struggle in Syria. JN, the al-Qaeda affiliate in Syria, counts many Jordanians in its ranks, including Mustafa Abdel-Latif, the brother-in-law of the late AQI leader Abu Musab al-Zarqawi. The flow of weaponry could also be reversed across the Syrian-Jordanian border. In October 2012, Jordanian intelligence dismantled an al-Qaeda cell readying attacks against Western interests, shopping areas and other soft targets in Amman.

Thus, the Jordanian calculation evolved as the conflict in Syria expanded. At first unwilling to allow the use of its territory and its border for operations aimed at destabilising Assad, the worsening refugee crisis, the potential use or loss of Syrian chemical weapons, the radicalisation of the opposition and the realisation that a long conflict would only increase the costs to Jordan have changed initial calculations.

Israel: the end of a predictable relationship

Locked since 1974 in a relatively predictable relationship with the Assad regime, Israel has demonstrated deep anxiety over the unrest in Syria. However aggressive Syrian policy under Assad was, Israel's conventional military superiority and a sense that the Assad regime recognised its own limitations and the strategic environment had made for fairly stable relations. In years prior to the uprising, the strengthening of the alliance with Iran, concern about Hizbullah's growing power in Lebanon and the realisation that Assad was engaging in more risk-taking (notably, the building of a nuclear reactor) led many in the Israeli establishment to favour quiet outreach to Damascus in the hope that it would counteract Assad's attachment to Tehran. This included peace talks under Turkish mediation that floundered in late 2008.

The eruption of the Syrian uprising compounded an already complicated strategic picture for Israel. The uprisings that hit the Arab world have profoundly affected its immediate neighbourhood. The downfall of Mubarak, the subsequent coming to power of the MB and questioning of the Camp David Accords in Egypt added considerable uncertainty to what had been a stable security partnership. Iran, meanwhile, wasted no time proclaiming the victory of Islamist ideals throughout the Arab world and sending warships through the Suez Canal and into the eastern Mediterranean. Jordan, the only other Arab state at peace with Israel, was also affected as widespread discontent with the Hashemite monarchy compounded the new assertiveness of the country's own Islamist opposition.

The uprising was initially greeted with a sense that Assad would prevail over a disparate and more radical opposition. For Israel, the strategic upside of the uprising – the weakening of the Iran-led resistance axis – was balanced by deep apprehension of the unknown. In Israeli eyes, Assad had always operated within acceptable parameters and shared Israel's concerns towards radical Islamist groups. The defence establishment was especially unwilling to part with a known rival that could be contained and deterred, especially as it faced profound changes in its relationship with Egypt.

By late 2011, the potency of the challenge and the consequences of the escalation by Assad forced a revision of Israeli assessments. Defense Minister Ehud Barak called the potential fall of Assad a 'blessing for the Middle East'.[37] In June 2012, President Shimon Peres, who was the first official to call for Assad to resign in July 2011, reiterated his call: 'There is reluctance to remove President Assad because they don't know what the alternative is. But Assad is no longer an alternative – he is finished. He cannot be an alternative, neither from a human point of view nor from a political point of view.'[38]

A number of factors explain the Israeli reassessment. Firstly, a weakened Assad was no longer as predictable and easy to deter. A comment from his cousin Rami Makhlouf in May 2011 raised concern: 'If there is no stability here, there's no way there will be stability in Israel. No way, and nobody can guarantee what will happen after, God forbid, anything happens to this regime.'[39] Ostensibly meant to remind the international community of the strategic certainty Assad offered, the comment also alluded to the possibility that Assad could provoke Israel to divert attention from his internal challenge. Assad did indeed prove to be increasingly less risk-averse. In 2011, for the first time since 1974, his forces allowed Palestinian refugees to demonstrate on the usually off-limits Golan Heights and breach the border, leading to deadly Israeli retaliation. In 2012, firefights and military movements occurred on the Golan Heights, prompting Israel to put its units on alert and return fire.

Secondly, there were considerable concerns over Syria's chemical arsenal. The risk that Assad would transfer these weapons to Hizbullah or that unknown rebel groups would seize them figured prominently in Israeli discussions with Washington.[40] Israel also feared that Assad would provide advanced game-changing weapon systems, such as anti-aircraft weaponry, from his own arsenal, and, in January 2013, an arms shipment allegedly carrying this type of weaponry to Hizbullah was destroyed by the Israeli air force inside Syria.

Thirdly was the fear, publicly acknowledged by the IDF, that the descent of Syria into civil strife could also prompt a massive refugee crisis on the Golan Heights. Its proximity to Alawite and Druze villages plus the short distance to Damascus (60km), suggested a possible influx of Syrians fleeing combat or retribution, a contingency for which Israel had to plan at a political, military and humanitarian level.

Fourthly, Israeli analysts recognised that the longer the struggle lasted, the more serious the consequences would be for Israel. The prospect of a fragmented Syria, with no central government to oversee its vast conventional capabilities and chemical arsenal or to control its territory or borders, called for new contingency planning. Israel had little knowledge of the armed groups springing up across Syria and feared that Salafi groups, such as JN, would operate in lawless areas close to the Golan Heights. Such groups, harder to identify and deter, could well prove more inclined to use force against Israel. In essence, the strategic certainty that characterised Syrian-Israeli relations is being replaced by uncertainty about the new Syrian actors, their agendas and their risk profiles.

This explains why Israel adopted a relatively low profile in dealing with the Syrian crisis, which it viewed as an Arab and international responsibility that required Israeli action only if Israeli security was directly affected. It has pressured Western governments to deny Syrian rebels man-portable air-defence systems (MANPADs) for fear they would end up in the hands of Salafis or Hizbullah, eroding Israeli air dominance.

The net benefit for Israel of the fall of Assad would be the ideological, political and military weakening of the rejectionist front led by Iran, whose influence in the Levant has exacerbated

Israeli fears about its nuclear programme. The Syrian uprising has already affected Tehran's standing among Arabs and could well deny it a base for operations. However, a protracted conflict would allow Iran to build networks across Syria to compensate, if not completely, for the loss of Assad and to organise new logistical lines to supply Hizbullah.

Israel may well calculate that a new government in Syria would necessarily break ties with Iran, in keeping with Syrian opposition leaders' statements to this effect in late 2011, and adopt a less confrontational stance towards the Jewish state, in line with the Gulf states and Turkey. However, it remains highly unlikely that any new government would relinquish the Syrian claim over the occupied Golan Heights. In fact, victorious rebel factions may be more likely to break from the stability enforced by Assad as a way to legitimise their armed status and mount resistance attacks against Israel on the Golan Heights.

Notes

1 Shibley Telhami, 'Annual Arab Public Opinion Survey 2010', University of Maryland with Zogby International, available at: http://www.brookings.edu/~/media/research/files/reports/2010/8/05%20arab%20opinion%20poll%20telhami/0805_arabic_opinion_poll_telhami.pdf.

2 Piotr Zalewski, 'Why Syria and Turkey Are Suddenly Far Apart on Arab Spring Protests', Time, 26 May 2011, http://www.time.com/time/world/article/0,8599,2074165,00.html.

3 Scott MacLeod, 'The Cairo Review Interview: Strategic Thinking', The Cairo Review of Global Affairs, 12 March 2012, http://www.aucegypt.edu/gapp/cairoreview/pages/articleDetails.aspx?aid=143.

4 Hilal Khashan, 'Saad Hariri's Moment of Truth', The Middle East Quarterly, Winter 2011, pp. 65–71.

5 Hokayem, 'Hizballah and Syria: Outgrowing the Proxy Relationship', The Washington Quarterly, Spring 2007, pp. 35–52.

6 Hokayem, 'The Gulf States and Syria', Brief for the United States Institute of Peace, November 2011, http://www.usip.org/publications/the-gulf-states-and-syria.

7 'Erdogan: Assad is a good friend, but he delayed reform efforts', Today's Zaman, 12 May 2011, http://www.todayszaman.com/news-243660-erdogan-assad-is-a-good-friend-but-he-delayed-reform-efforts.html.

8 See editorials in Al-Watan, a daily newspaper owned by Rami

Makhlouf, including a May 2011 opinion piece that lambasts Erdogan's 'arrogant "reformatory preaching"'. 'Rami Makhlouf's daily blasts Turkey; Draws MB link', *The Mideastwire Blog*, http://mideastwire.wordpress.com/2011/05/12/rami-makhloufs-daily-blasts-turkey-draws-mb-link/.

9 'Saudi Arabia calls for Syrian reforms', *Al-Jazeera English*, 8 August 2011, http://www.aljazeera.com/news/middleeast/2011/08/201187213922184761.html.

10 'Syria's oppressors will not survive', *Today's Zaman*, 16 September 2011, http://www.todayszaman.com/news-256939-turkeys-erdogan-in-libya-as-sirte-battle-rages.html.

11 'Qatar FM calls on Syria to stop "killing machine" as Arab League meeting ends', *Al Arabiya News*, 13 September 2011, http://www.alarabiya.net/articles/2011/09/13/166617.html.

12 'Policy of Zero Problems with our Neighbors', Turkish Ministry of Foreign Affairs, http://www.mfa.gov.tr/policy-of-zero-problems-with-our-neighbors.en.mfa.

13 For more on regional fears over a 'Shia crescent', see: Robin Wright and Peter Baker, 'Iraq, Jordan See Threat to Election from Iran', 8 December 2004, *The Washington Post*, http://www.washingtonpost.com/wp-dyn/articles/A43980-2004Dec7.html.

14 Asma Alsharif and Amena Bakr, 'Saudi steers citizens away from Syrian "jihad"', Reuters, 12 September 2012, http://www.reuters.com/article/2012/09/12/us-saudi-syria-jihad-idUSBRE88B0XY20120912.

15 'Saudi religious authority forbids "jihad" in Syria', *Alakhbar English*, 7 June 2012, http://english.al-akhbar.com/node/8198.

16 Ruth Sherlock, 'Syria 'names 142 foreign jihadists who fought with rebels', *The Telegraph*, 27 November 2012, http://www.telegraph.co.uk/news/worldnews/middleeast/syria/9706777/Syria-names-142-foreign-jihadists-who-fought-with-rebels.html.

17 Ian Black and Julian Borger, 'Gulf states warned against arming Syrian rebels', *Guardian*, 5 April 2012, http://www.guardian.co.uk/world/2012/apr/05/gulf-states-warning-arming-syria.

18 Robert F. Worth, 'Citing U.S. Fears, Arab Allies Limit Syrian Rebel Aid', *The New York Times*, 6 October 2012, http://www.nytimes.com/2012/10/07/world/middleeast/citing-us-fears-arab-allies-limit-aid-to-syrian-rebels.html?pagewanted=all.

19 Rania Abouzeid, 'Syria's Secular and Islamist Rebels: Who Are the Saudis and the Qataris Arming?', *Time Magazine*, 18 September 2012, http://world.time.com/2012/09/18/syrias-secular-and-islamist-rebels-who-are-the-saudis-and-the-qataris-arming/.

20 Nour Malas and Margaret Coker, 'Jordan Said to Help Arm Syria Rebels', *The Wall Street Journal*, 9 November 2012, http://online.wsj.com/article/SB10001424127887323894704578104853961999838.html?mod=wsj_share_tweet.

21 'Supreme Leader's View of Islamic Awakening', The Centre for Preserving and Publishing the Works of Grand Ayatollah Sayyid Ali Khamenei, 19 May 2011,

http://english.khamenei.ir/index.php?option=com_content&task=view&id=1458&Itemid=13.

22 Farnaz Fassihi, 'Iran said to send troops to bolster Syria', *The Wall Street Journal*, 27 August 2012, http://online.wsj.com/article/SB10000872396390444230504577615393756632230.html.

23 'Khamenei blames US, Israel for Syria civil war', *The Times of Israel*, 25 October 2012, http://www.timesofisrael.com/ayatollah-ali-khamenei-blames-us-israel-for-syria-civil-war/.

24 'Bashar Assad, Iran's red line: Velayati', *Press TV*, 20 January 2013, http://www.presstv.com/detail/2013/01/20/284641/bashar-assad-irans-red-line-velayati/.

25 'PKK receiving Iranian support: Turkish interior minister', *Hurriyet Daily News*, 26 November 2012, http://www.hurriyetdailynews.com/pkk-receiving-iranian-support-turkish-interior-minister.aspx?pageID=238&nID=35473&NewsCatID=338.

26 Gul Tuysuz, 'Turkey to Syria: Don't send arms through our air space', *CNN*, 12 October 2012, http://edition.cnn.com/2012/10/11/world/meast/syria-civil-war/index.html.

27 For a detailed analysis of Maliki's consolidation of power, see: Toby Dodge, *Iraq: From War to a New Authoritarianism* (Abingdon: Routledge for the IISS, 2012).

28 Nicholas Blanford, 'Video appears to show Hezbollah and Iraqi Shiites fighting in Syria', *Christian Science Monitor*, 18 January 2013, http://www.csmonitor.com/World/Middle-East/2013/0118/Video-appears-to-show-Hezbollah-and-Iraqi-Shiites-fighting-in-Syria.

29 'Miqati Says Cabinet Committed to Policy of Disassociation, Receiving Aid for Refugees Has Become Urgent', *Naharnet*, 26 January 2013, 'http://www.naharnet.com/stories/en/69839.

30 The most serious incident occurred in the Bekaa town of Arsal in February 2003, when Lebanese army personnel arrested a man accused of helping Syrian rebels. Arsal residents confronted them and killed two soldiers. Ann Maria Luca, 'What really happened in Arsal?', *NowLebanon*, 6 February 2013, https://now.mmedia.me/lb/en/reportsfeatures/what-really-happened-in-arsal.

31 Fielding-Smith, 'Syrian Influx is cold comfort for Lebanon', *Financial Times*, 24 September 2012, http://www.ft.com/cms/s/0/f70564a2-0635-11e2-a28a-00144feabdco.html#axzz2PDdZke6p.

32 Liz Sly, 'Syrian refugees overwhelm Lebanon, region', *The Washington Post*, 23 January 2013, http://www.washingtonpost.com/world/middle_east/syria-refugees-overwhelm-lebanon-region/2013/01/22/baoc1af8-60d7-11e2-bc4f-1f06fffb7acf_story.html.

33 Blanford, 'Accusations mount of Hezbollah's fighting in Syria', *The Christian Science Monitor*, 15 October 2012, http://www.csmonitor.com/World/Middle-East/2012/1015/Accusations-mount-of-Hezbollah-fighting-in-Syria.

34 'Reports: Hizbullah Commander, Several Fighters Killed in Homs', *Naharnet*, 2 October 2012, http://www.naharnet.com/stories/en/55639.

35 Blanford, 'Video appears to show Hezbollah and Iraqi Shiites fighting in Syria'.

36 See data on Syrian refugees from the UNHCR's Inter-agency Information Sharing Portal: http://data.unhcr.org/syrianrefugees/country.php?id=107.

37 Amos Harel, 'Ehud Barak in Vienna: Assad's downfall will be "blessing for the Middle East"', *Haaretz*, 12 December 2011, http://www.haaretz.com/print-edition/news/ehud-barak-in-vienna-assad-s-downfall-will-be-blessing-for-the-middle-east-1.400880.

38 Lally Weymouth, '"Not a Threat – More Than a Threat"', *Slate*, 15 June 2012, http://www.slate.com/articles/news_and_politics/foreigners/2012/06/israeli_president_shimon_peres_on_iran_syria_president_assad_and_the_egyptian_crisis_.html.

39 Anthony Shadid, 'Syrian Elite to Fight Protests to '"the End"', *The New York Times*, 10 May 2011, http://www.nytimes.com/2011/05/11/world/middleeast/11makhlouf.html?pagewanted=all&_r=0.

40 Helene Cooper, 'Washington Begins to Plan for Collapse of Syrian Government', *The New York Times*, 18 July 2012, http://www.nytimes.com/2012/07/19/world/middleeast/washington-begins-to-plan-for-collapse-of-syrian-government.html?pagewanted=all.

CHAPTER FIVE

Syria in the international context

The outbreak of the Syrian revolution followed, and was undoubtedly inspired by, momentous events across the region. The Arab uprisings that swept Tunisia, Egypt, Libya, Bahrain and Yemen from December 2010 had already shaken long-held assumptions about the stability and resilience of authoritarian regimes, sending confused Arab and non-Arab policymakers scrambling for adequate responses. Both the region's political culture and order seemed on the verge of upheaval.

Even then, initial international assessments downplayed the potential for Egypt-style political turbulence. *Washington Post* columnist David Ignatius reflected this mainstream view in early February 2011: '... Assad today is less vulnerable than Mubarak: His regime is at least as corrupt and autocratic, but it has remained steadfastly anti-American and anti-Israel. Hard as it is for us in the West to accept, this rejectionism adds to Assad's power, whereas Mubarak is diminished by his image as the West's puppet.'[1]

To many governments and analysts, the failure of a first protest in mid-February, in the souks of Damascus, to gather momentum suggested that a particular mix of factors would decisively work in the Assad regime's favor.[2] Echoing the 'old guard-new guard' misconception (discussed in Chapter One), observers believed that government reformers would seize the opportunity to push for political reforms. This assessment held that constitutional amendments and limited political change ahead of national elections scheduled for 2011 would be enough to placate popular dissatisfaction.

Conversely, the example of Libya was seen as a deterrent to would-be revolutionaries in Syria. The massive use of force by Gadhafi seemed more likely to be replicated by Assad if challenged, than easing out of power as Tunisian and Egyptian Presidents Ben Ali and Mubarak did. Furthermore, Syrian society, widely seen as docile, wary of nearby sectarian strife and still traumatised by the 1982 Hama episode, was judged to lack the will to embark on a revolution that would cost it dearly.

The world was looking the other way when Syria's revolutionary tremors began to shake the country in March 2011. As protests broke out in Deraa, the Gulf states intervened in Bahrain to help the Sunni Al-Khalifah monarchy quell the uprising led by the Shia-dominated opposition, and the UNSC approved Resolution 1973 authorising 'all necessary measures' to protect Libyan civilians against the forces of Muammar Gadhafi. Meanwhile, the largest demonstration to date and mass resignations and defections took place in Yemen, and Egyptians voted in a constitutional referendum that was seen as the first legal step in the country's post-Mubarak transition. Combined, these events made the unrest in the mid-sized, rural Syrian city of Deraa seem both minor and unwelcome. In the words of a Western diplomat in Syria, it was perceived primarily as an 'irritant'.[3]

Western confusion and ambivalence

The first few months of Syria's revolution exposed the confusion and ambivalence of Western states regarding Syria, a disposition that would colour their attitude and response during the first two years of the uprising.

From a certain standpoint, the timing of the uprising had been most unfortunate. Western states had just begun to rebuild relations with the Assad regime after several years of tension over Syria's interference in Lebanon and Iraq, sponsorship of various radical groups, covert nuclear programme and alliance with Iran. Western governments assessed that the policy of isolation had failed to reorient and constrain Syrian foreign policy. Syria's improving relations with Turkey, secret negotiations with Israel and enduring alliance with Iran suggested to them that another, more accommodating approach toward Assad was needed. Having spent significant political capital and energy in the process of reaching out to Assad, they seemed reluctant to write off this investment.

In particular, the Obama administration had made engagement with Syria an essential element of its Middle East strategy. Breaking with the confrontational approach of the Bush administration (which had left Syria out of its 'Axis of Evil' but later tried to isolate it through bilateral and multilateral action), Obama shifted course and actively courted Bashar al-Assad. Obama's electoral promise to withdraw US troops from Iraq, his stated desire to reactivate a moribund peace process between Israelis and Palestinians and overall foreign-policy philosophy shaped his Middle East strategy. As a result, Obama's Middle East peace envoy, George Mitchell, and other senior administration officials repeatedly visited Damascus. Senator John Kerry, then the powerful chairman of the US Senate Foreign Relations Committee, became the administration's point man, travelling to the Syrian capital several times to meet Assad and engage in quiet, direct diplomacy, aimed primarily at jump-starting peace talks with Israel. A significant step came in 2010 with the appointment of a US ambassador to Syria, despite strong objections by Republican senators and after a five-year hiatus (the Bush administration had withdrawn its ambassador in 2005 over suspected Syrian involvement in the assassination of former Lebanese Prime Minister Rafik Hariri).

European governments had preceded the US on the road to Damascus. Some EU countries had always been sceptical of the merits of isolating Syria, but France, Germany and the United Kingdom had pushed this policy through in 2005, and it had lasted until late 2007. It unravelled spectacularly when French President Nicolas Sarkozy, who had succeeded the staunchly anti-Assad Jacques Chirac in 2007, hosted Assad in Paris in July 2008. The Syrian-French rapprochement, motivated by Sarkozy's desire to break with the Chirac legacy and conduct an ambitious Mediterranean agenda, set a new tone for other European states that then rushed to the Syrian capital.

From the 1990s, the European strategy was to entangle Syria in a web of norms, agreements and initiatives aimed at moderating and reorienting its foreign policy over time.[4] European states, either independently or collectively, approached Syria primarily through the prism of the Arab–Israeli conflict and its impact on regional security. Despite earnest efforts by the European Commission to bring coherence and discipline to EU policy in its immediate neighbourhood, a common strategy towards Syria remained more of an aspiration than a reality. This affected the articulation and prioritisation of EU interests regarding Syria: some countries placed high emphasis on human rights and political reform, while most, including more powerful states, were reluctant to do so out of pragmatism, expediency or economic interest. Moreover, except for the rare occasions when consensus reigned, EU influence over Syria amounted to considerably less than the sum of the influence of each of its members. These divisions meant that EU influence on Syria's domestic and security policies was marginal, and also allowed Syria to pit European countries against each other.[5]

This is best illustrated by the tortuous, and eventually failed, attempt to conclude an association agreement between the EU and Syria. The economic and trade benefits dangled by the EU and seen to support the process of economic reform failed to sway the Syrian leadership, which worried that the political and economic conditions and restrictive language on weapons of mass destruction would constrain its margin of manoeuvre. Ultimately, therefore, the strategic and political costs of partnering with the EU were deemed too great, and prevented implementation of the economic and reform imperatives necessary to secure an agreement.

By 2010, Western rapprochement with Syria had delivered few tangible and sustainable returns. Syrian political influence in Iraq turned out to have been overestimated as US and Iraqi forces managed to dismantle insurgent networks. The détente in Lebanon came at the price of an uncomfortable recognition of Syrian influence there. Syria rebuffed requests by the International Atomic Energy Agency (IAEA) to inspect its suspected nuclear facilities following the 2007 destruction of the Kibar nuclear reactor by the Israeli air force.

Western states were nevertheless unwilling to reverse course. Syria was no longer seen as a major strategic problem but as one that could be managed through diplomacy. Importantly, Arab states too had joined the engagement bandwagon, with Saudi Arabia brokering a new *entente* over Lebanon in 2010 with Damascus, while an assertive Turkey increasingly positioned itself as Syria's regional and international mentor.

It is also important that Western rapprochement with Assad gave little priority to issues of political reform and human rights, as linking democratic conditions to regional security concerns had come to be seen as naïve and counterproductive. The experience of Iraq, the perceived loss of credibility in the Arab world and a general aversion to advocating domestic matters led the US administration to privilege state-to-state relations.

All these factors help to explain why the initial European and US reaction to the uprising betrayed a lack of knowledge of

Syrian society beyond Damascus elite circles, as well as how they came to an unrealistically optimistic assessment of the regime's readiness to reform. A forward-looking Assad was seen to be pitted against a backward-looking regime and was, at the very least, a known quantity in the absence of obvious alternatives. Working on the assumption that the president could be dissociated from his regime (discarding the fact that the former headed and was embedded in the latter), it was said that Assad's trump card would be to mount a coup against his own regime.

Statements encouraging reforms and expressing confidence in Assad's willingness and ability to heed calls for political change were the first response from Western governments. In a 16 March speech at the Washington-based Carnegie Endowment for International Peace, Kerry best reflected this widely-held view: '[Assad] understands what's going on. [Syria] is a secular country. And I guarantee you he's committed to trying to stay secular, if the rest of the world will sort of help to make that possible.' He emphasised: 'My judgment is that Syria will move; Syria will change, as it embraces a legitimate relationship with the United States and the West and economic opportunity that comes with it and the participation that comes with it.'[6] Then Secretary of State Clinton confirmed this assessment weeks later: 'There's a different leader in Syria now. Many of the members of Congress of both parties who have gone to Syria in recent months have said they believe [Assad] is a reformer.'[7] Clinton refuted comparisons between the then ongoing war in Libya, where Gadhafi '[called in] aircraft and indiscriminately [strafed and bombed his] own cities', and Syria, where 'police actions [had] exceeded the use of force. Each of these situations are [sic] unique.'[8]

An incremental response

In the early months of the uprising, official Western pronouncements stopped short of calling for the resignation of Assad. This dovetailed the position of the Gulf states and Turkey, who also preferred to encourage Assad to enact reforms and reach out to the opposition. The onus was placed on Assad, who was said to have a choice between repression and political change. Clinton called on Assad to 'respond to the demands of the people by a process of credible and inclusive democratic change'.[9] He was expected, in the words of President Obama in May 2011, to 'lead that transition, or get out of the way'.[10] As late as June 2011, the US ambassador to Syria, Robert Ford, stated that the US government supported 'dialogue between the Syrian government and the opposition inside [Syria], in order to formulate a political framework that paves the way to ending the crisis in the country'.[11]

This tentative and wishful Western response in the early days was due to perplexity and fatigue with Arab political unrest, but also due to deficient knowledge of and reporting from Syria. The spread of the uprising from the backwater of Deraa to other, often unknown parts of Syria came as a surprise, as did its overwhelmingly peaceful and organic nature in cities like Hama and Homs. There, new and largely unknown leaderships and networks were emerging, pushing for a peaceful transition of power. Elsewhere, it was difficult to make sense of the dynamics. In particular, the intense fighting in May 2011 in Tal Kalakh, on the Syrian-Lebanese border, and in June of the same year in Jisr al-Shughour, on the Syrian-Turkish border, hinted to other factors at play.

The magnitude and vigour of the peaceful anti-regime demonstrations, the brutality and extent of the security response, and the limited political proposals put forward by Assad combined to alter Western assessments of the trajectory of events in Syria. Increased diplomatic contacts with a wider section of Syrian society, including revolutionary activists and a controversial visit in July 2011 by the French and American ambassadors to Hama, where fears of the repeat of the 1982 massacre were manifest, contributed to this shift. By the summer of 2011, an understanding crystallised in Western capitals that the revolution would seriously challenge the pillars of Assad's power and that the Syrian leader would meet this challenge with brutal force.

This shift in attitude was evident in the declarations of Western officials. France proved particularly vocal, probably prompted by a sense of frustration given Sarkozy's closeness to Assad in previous years, while, in August 2011, Obama issued a statement marking this policy change: 'For the sake of the Syrian people, the time has come for President Assad to step aside.'[12] Even then, the US remained attached to the notion of a peaceful transition that would preserve the Syrian state and bring about a soft-landing, and so Western states prioritised diplomacy. Their Arab, Turkish and also Russian interlocutors were believed to maintain access and credibility with important contacts inside the Assad regime that would be willing, with the right incentives and under negotiated circumstances, to pave the way for a transition.

In parallel, Western states adopted a series of measures to pressure the top echelons of the regime and squeeze the regime's resources. The objective was to encourage defections of senior government and security officials in the expectation that this would fracture and debilitate the regime. Sanctions and public discussion about a possible referral of senior Syrian officials to the International Criminal Court (ICC) alongside offers of safe haven and intelligence outreach were intended to generate additional incentives to would-be defectors. As early as April 2011, the US and the EU began to adopt targeted financial sanctions against dozens of Syrian officials and businessmen involved in the repression. They also imposed trade and oil export sanctions to degrade the regime's financial resources and in the hope that, by attaching a high financial cost for continued support of Assad, Syria's powerful business community would abandon the regime.

Western governments were not optimistic about Assad's capacity to survive, and officials regularly measured his time left in office in weeks or months. Fred Hof, a senior US official, said in December 2011 that Assad was 'a dead man walking'.[13] Ultimately, this sense of the inevitability of Assad's demise and the emphasis on non-military tools considerably underestimated the regime's resilience and misread Syrian dynamics, both contributing to and justifying Western complacency about the real costs of removing Assad.

Furthermore, given their focus on Libya, Western countries were relieved and content to encourage the initial mediation efforts of Turkey and the Arab states in the early days of the uprising. Reliance on these regional players quickly emerged as a key pillar of Western policy, as they provided legitimacy, political cover, indirect channels into the Syrian regime, contacts with the Syrian opposition and escalatory options. Given their history of antagonism with Syria, Western states calculated that a regional face would dispel Arab and Syrian suspicions that the West was seeking to manufacture or manipulate the uprising – it would blunt expected criticism that they were motivated by imperialist anti-Muslim motives. Thus, Western strategy was to back the Gulf states as they set the diplomatic pace and to spend political capital on mobilising the international community against the Assad regime.

As Syria's closest allies besides Iran, Qatar and Turkey were expected to carry unique influence in Damascus and the ability to sway Assad towards negotiations. The strategic interests and growing assertiveness of the Gulf states, best exemplified by their support of the Libya intervention but also by the deployment of Gulf Cooperation Council (GCC) troops in Bahrain, made them pivotal players as well. From a Western perspective, the Gulf, principally Saudi Arabia, Qatar and the UAE, could deploy muscle in important arenas (notably the Arab League and the Organisation of Islamic Cooperation); controlled powerful media tools that could shape narratives and perceptions; and could mobilise significant resources.

Western governments did, however, question the Gulf states' vision for Syria's future, as well as their ability to operate in Syria without fanning sectarian flames or inviting backlash. Of particular concern was their disposition to promote Islamist groups that were largely unknown and often worrisome to Western officials. Engagement with the Gulf states, therefore, was also aimed to monitor and shape their activities in Syria, and their different agendas.

By the late summer of 2011, the break between Ankara, Doha and Damascus required new assessments and strategies, however. This served to illustrate the very intransigence of Assad, but also shifted more responsibility onto Western shoulders.

Another component of Western policy was to work through the UN. The Obama administration came to power with the intention to deal with crises through multilateral institutions and share the burden of conflict management with regional countries and organisations. This was especially the case in the Middle East, where the costs of involvement, in terms of US standing and perception, remained high. The management of the Libyan crisis through the Arab League, the UN and NATO, with minimally visible US fingerprints, was seen as a satisfactory template. Ironically, the Libya precedent made it more difficult to contemplate serious action on Syria: the size and complexity of the Syria challenge surpassed that of Libya and there was little appetite for a repetition.

International diplomacy

The Arab League initiative

The failure of Turkish and Gulf leaders throughout the summer of 2011 to convince Assad to embark on a genuine reformist course and the escalation of the violence in the autumn pushed the Syrian crisis onto the agenda of the Arab League.

Freshly vindicated by their success against the Gadhafi regime, the Gulf states sought to utilise the Arab League, which had legitimised the NATO-led intervention in Libya, as an instrument of pressure. With Egypt mired in its complex transition and a temporary absence of traditionally sovereignty-sensitive Arab states such as Algeria and Yemen, Saudi Arabia and Qatar (at that time holder of the rotating presidency of the ministerial committee of the Arab League) found new diplomatic space.

In October 2011, the Arab League adopted a resolution condemning violence and urging immediate dialogue, which was endorsed by the UNSC. The Syrian government reluctantly committed to this peace plan, aimed at ending the bloodshed, and high-level Arab diplomats reached out to the newly formed SNC and the regime to jump-start political talks.

Within weeks, however, after the Syrian government failed to abide by its obligations under this plan, the Arab League took the symbolic step of suspending Syria's membership in the organisation. It also adopted trade and financial sanctions against Syria and a freeze on government assets, and imposed travel bans on senior officials. The most significant outcome was to isolate the Assad regime further, even if the political willingness and the capability to enforce these sanctions was lacking in many Arab countries. Tellingly, Lebanon opposed this, while Iraq abstained.

In mid-December 2011, the Arab League deployed an observer mission charged with monitoring the implementation of its plan. The observers catalogued the regime's massive use of violence and also reported on the increasing militarisation of the opposition. However, under-staffed and badly equipped, this mission was not taken seriously by either side and the violence endured. By mid-January, the wisdom of sending in monitors was being questioned by Syrian revolutionaries and the Gulf states announced they would withdraw their observers that same month, effectively ending the mission. Meanwhile, an

attempt by the Arab League to broker a national unity government in January 2012 was denounced by the Syrian government
as 'a blatant intervention in its sovereign affairs'.[14]

By late January 2012, the Arab League peace plan had been
undone by the ineffectiveness of its monitoring mission, the
duplicity of Assad over dialogue and the Syrian opposition's
own divisions and contradictions – the SNC had initially rejected
the monitoring mission, calling for international intervention in
the form of a safe zone.

The shaky Arab League consensus on Syria, until then enforced
by the Gulf states, was increasingly challenged by a growing
number of Arab states that disapproved of their interventionist
stance and the insistence on obtaining Assad's departure. Arab
divisions were further exposed as the chairmanship of the Arab
League passed on to Iraq, and Prime Minister Maliki increasingly found common ground with Assad.

The recourse to the UN
Consequently the Syrian file was fully referred to the UNSC,
opening a new phase of international diplomacy. (A draft resolution under Chapter 41 threatening sanctions against the Syrian
government had already been vetoed by Russia in October 2011.)
Moving the management of the Syrian crisis to the UN put a
greater burden on the shoulders of the great powers, which had
so far encouraged a regionally brokered solution.

Russia and China were under pressure to demonstrate that
they could do more than shield their ally from international
wrath – that they could also moderate and nudge Syria towards
dialogue. US, European and Arab governments had to reconcile
their own indecision with diplomatic theatrics while navigat-
ing the contradictory demands and expectations of the Syrian
opposition. The legacy of the NATO intervention in Libya still
hung over the UNSC, as Russia and China felt the campaign
had gone beyond its UN mandate, while the presence of rising

powers sceptical about the merits of pressure and intervention (India and South Africa served in 2011–2013; Brazil in 2010–2012) further complicated UN politics in New York.

Early February 2012 saw the first UN deliberations that essentially sought to add coercive power and international muscle to the Arab League initiative. A draft resolution, which was toned down to obtain Russian approval, demanded an end to violence, the liberation of political prisoners, the launch of an inclusive political process and the holding of elections. It also called on Assad to transfer his powers to his vice-president during the transition process. Despite Western and Arab attempts to coax and shame them, Russia and China vetoed it, on the grounds that it placed disproportionate responsibility and blame on the Assad regime. This move, seen by many Syrians as a licence for Assad to increase his repression, caused Arab and Western outrage. The Gulf states and their Western allies pushed for and obtained a non-binding resolution by the UN General Assembly in mid-February 2012, backing the initiative.[15]

With international diplomacy grinding to a halt, the UN and the Arab League joined forces to appoint former UN Secretary-General Kofi Annan as their envoy to Syria, in late February. Annan was tasked with mediating between world and regional powers and plotting a transitional process. In March, he put forward a six-point peace plan that expanded on the Arab League initiative – including the provision of humanitarian assistance – and proposed the deployment of a UN mission to enforce its implementation. Annan came under criticism for engaging Assad in a diplomatic process that was seen to offer him space and time to continue his repression – he was absent at several Friends of Syria meetings and was shunned by Saudi Arabia.

In April, the UN mission started its operations. While better staffed and trained than its ill-fated Arab League predecessor, it still was short on personnel and lacked adequate equipment and transport. Despite their limited mandate, international observers were at first welcomed by Syrian activists and they were able to investigate several instances of human-rights abuses, including the Houla massacre for which they blamed government militias. However, violence and concerns that observers would be targeted curtailed their operational freedom and safety, and the mission was suspended in August 2012.

Meanwhile, in June 2012, at the initiative of Annan, the secretaries-general of the UN and the Arab League, and the foreign ministers of the US, the UK, France, China, Russia, Turkey, Iraq, Kuwait and Qatar, met in Geneva and adopted a plan for dialogue and a negotiated transition.[16] Although Western states failed to obtain a binding UNSC resolution to bolster the Geneva plan, due to Russian and Chinese opposition, this new plan became the focus of international diplomacy. While Annan called for a 'managed but full change of government',[17] the plan effectively postponed addressing the main hurdle: the fate of Assad. The Syrian opposition, backed by its Arab supporters, insisted that any transition be preceded by the resignation of the Syrian president, while Western states seemed amenable to Assad transferring all his executive powers to his vice-president ahead of inclusive political talks (dubbed the Yemen option) and later to a transitional governing body. Russia and China opposed any such preconditions. In later months, the discussion over Assad's fate expanded to include whether a transition should allow him to finish his term up to 2014 or to run in any future election, and whether he (and the top tier of his clique) should be offered safe exit, asylum and immunity.

Annan left his position as joint envoy in August 2012, blaming regional and international powers for the failure of his efforts. The veteran Algerian diplomat Lakhdar Brahimi replaced him, banking on changing circumstances (including a military stalemate), revised calculations (Russian rethinking and Arab mellowing) and the increasing cost of the Syrian conflict to revive the Geneva plan. Indeed, Brahimi warned that

Syria faced two paths: his plan or 'hell'.[18] Brahimi floated the idea of forming a transitional government to oversee the presidential election scheduled for 2014, allowing Assad to remain as a ceremonial president until then, but this failed to garner any real support.

There have been several key stumbling blocks for the various efforts at resolving the crisis on the international stage. Firstly, diplomacy had become decoupled from events on the ground and was undermined by the behaviour of regional foes and allies of Assad. Rapidly-changing dynamics on the ground, regional disinterest in a negotiated solution and great power politics have hampered international diplomacy. The sense that the outcome inevitably meant the political end of either side and that the momentum had decisively shifted in the rebels' favour in the second half of 2012 made the opposition less interested in a brokered solution, but also less capable of negotiations given its own fragmentation. While some civilian leaders favoured negotiations to pre-empt the rise of militias and jump-start an orderly transition, most armed commanders and many opposition leaders displayed intransigence. Meanwhile, Saudi Arabia, Qatar and Turkey, who were vocally calling for Assad's immediate exit from the autumn of 2011, proved especially opposed to a negotiated settlement; Riyadh particularly feared that such a process would create an opening for Iran.

Secondly, a united political opposition, to agree on the merits of talks and obtain the endorsement of the various political and rebel groups, would be essential but the SNC was both too divided and too weak to fulfill this task. By the time the more representative NC was formed, in November 2012, the already slim chances of a political resolution had considerably diminished.

Thirdly, much rode on Russia's ability and willingness to convince Assad to engage in genuine dialogue, but having derived lessons from the SNC's failed approaches towards

Moscow, the leadership of the NC appeared uninterested in engaging Russia. Furthermore, beyond Russia's own interests, its leverage over Assad was difficult to assess. In December 2012, Foreign Minister Sergei Lavrov said: '[Assad] has repeatedly said, both publicly and privately, including during his meeting with Lakhdar Brahimi not long ago, that he has no plans to go anywhere, that he will stay in his post until the end, that he will, as he says, protect the Syrian people, Syrian sovereignty and so forth. There is no possibility of changing this position.'[19] This admission of Russian limitations raised the question of the merits of pressuring Russia to obtain a UN resolution since it would probably not lead to concessions by Assad. As Assad retrenched in a fight for his survival, any Russian leverage would also probably have shrunk. Either way, a more negative Russian assessment of Assad's chances of survival would not necessarily translate into new policy, given Russia's principled opposition to any intervention or UN-sanctioned regime change.

Fourthly, the viability of a political solution rested on Assad's self-image as well as his own calculations and objectives. Since the beginning of the uprising, the Syrian leader gave no indication that he would leave the presidency, step aside or depart Syria to facilitate a transition. In his meetings with Russian and UN officials, he displayed no interest in a genuine political dialogue and argued that the political reforms he enacted in 2011 and 2012 sufficed. Rather, he saw the diplomatic process as a way to assert his continued relevance, without making significant concessions.

Finally, the mechanism and format of a political dialogue remains unclear. As the architect of the 1989 Taif Agreement that ended the Lebanese civil war, Brahimi could claim significant experience. Choreographing a similar process for Syria represented a considerably greater challenge given the geopolitics of the crisis. In Lebanon, the parties to the conflict were seeking adjustments to the political system rather than wholesale transformation; the local factions were exhausted; there was a regional and international consensus on ending the conflict; and Syria was the undisputed military hegemon. The situation in Syria as of late 2012 was fundamentally different: the various parties to the conflict sought total victory; the local factions were engaged in what they perceived as an existential struggle; regional and international powers had clashing interests and objectives; and there was no foreign occupier or superior military power. Thus, reaching an inclusive and applicable agreement over power sharing, minority rights, political reform, the state's identity, security reform, transitional justice and reconciliation through a mediation process have become less likely than ever.

The debate over the responsibility to protect

The escalation of the Syrian crisis led to calls for the activation of the concept of the responsibility to protect (R2P)[20], adopted by the UN General Assembly in 2005, which calls for collective action to prevent or end 'genocide, war crimes, ethnic cleansing and crimes against humanity'.[21] The debate over whether this should be applied gained momentum in light of Assad's resort to escalatory repression (air power, indiscriminate shelling, the destruction of major cities and the possible use of chemical weapons), as well as the magnitude of the humanitarian catastrophe (60,000 killed,[22] 460,000 refugees[23] and 2.5m IDPs[24] by late 2012 according to the UN), documented atrocities (for instance, a UN investigation blamed the regime's military and the Shabbiha for the Houla massacre[25]) and the prospects of sectarian cleansing.

The doctrine was seen by both its proponents and its critics as a way to bypass the deadlock at the UNSC and enact coercive action. Measures under R2P could encompass the adoption of sanctions, implementation of an arms embargo, referrals to the ICC, and, as a last resort, military options, including the imposition of safe and no-fly zones. However, obstinate Russian and

Chinese opposition, the lukewarm position of Western states towards military involvement, the risks of humanitarian intervention in an Arab country and questions about the legality of such action prevented a full examination of this path. By late 2012, the UN had yet to impose any kind of sanctions against the Assad regime.

The Friends of Syria process

Countries demanding the ouster of Assad devised a parallel track to shore up the Syrian opposition and to bypass the paralysed UNSC. The informal Group of Friends of the Syrian People gathered for the first time in Tunisia in late February 2012. This was followed by regular meetings in Istanbul, Paris and Marrakesh, attended by over 120 states.

Russia and China boycotted its proceedings, arguing that the exclusion of the Syrian government, the embrace of opposition groups sympathetic to the then-burgeoning armed rebellion and the insistence on Assad's departure further complicated a political solution and that the process could legitimise armed intervention outside international law. Some countries assumed a more ambiguous attitude: Iraq, for example, attended its meetings but refrained from adopting its positions.

The Friends of Syria process was designed primarily to nurture and empower the SNC, which it officially recognised as 'a legitimate representative' of the Syrian people in April 2012. Major Western and Arab supporters of the Syrian opposition saw the maturing and expansion of the SNC as a necessary condition to grant it exclusive recognition. Material international assistance was meant to buttress the SNC, but was also conditional on its progress.

Ultimately, however, this process exacerbated divisions among the supporters of the Syrian opposition and highlighted the lack of tangible policy and material commitment. Notably, Friends of Syria established no formal joint mechanism to coordinate material support, which reflected divisions among its members over the appropriate course of action. Some countries, like Saudi Arabia, felt that the support extended to the Syrian opposition fell short of expectations. Turkey hoped that the contact group could extend cover for a limited military intervention to create a safe zone or a no-fly zone. Others, notably the US, preferred not to make any commitment with direct security implications beyond their bilateral political and humanitarian help.

As fighting intensified in early 2012, the question of whether and how to arm and fund the emerging rebel groups took centre stage. Proponents of weaponisation argued that channeling support through the SNC would empower the group and also moderate and coordinate rebel units. (At the Istanbul meeting in April, Saudi Arabia, Qatar and the UAE announced the creation of a US$100m-dollar fund to pay the salaries of the rebel fighters.) The performance of the SNC fell well below expectations, however. The organisation was seen as not representative, competent or sufficiently proactive, and too beholden to its Turkish and Qatari patrons. Its internal operations proved opaque and dysfunctional, and there were concerns about its presumed Islamist orientation and the dominance of the MB.

Many countries, especially the US, had grown disappointed with the SNC, although it had staked its credibility on obtaining international recognition, funding and weaponry and on delivering international action. The failure to obtain strong UN action and Western hesitancy hurt an organisation seen by many Syrians as a foreign creation. The perception that the SNC had turned into a puppet of Qatari and Turkish policy further damaged its facade of autonomy from foreign interference. Moreover, its standing suffered from comparisons with Syrian-based groups: SNC members were disparaged as indulging in a life of luxury abroad and engaging in petty competition while rebels and activists risked their lives. It was only during the summer of 2012 that senior SNC members travelled to areas freed from Assad control.

Washington cooperated with disgruntled opposition members to shake-up the Syrian opposition and form the NC, in November 2012. The NC received exclusive recognition as the legitimate representative of the Syrian people at the Friends of Syria meeting in Marrakesh in December.

Making sense of Western hesitancy

Western states had long viewed Assad's Syria more as a manageable nuisance than a strategic threat, especially when compared to other Middle Eastern countries. Many Western policymakers harboured the hope that Syria could be eventually won over thanks to the right mix of incentives, regional integration and inclusion in the regional-security architecture. A sense that Syria pursued legitimate grievances through asymmetric means also pervaded their thinking: its security policy could be explained by the imbalance of power with Israel, which occupied the Golan Heights, and by aggressive US policy, especially during the George W. Bush years. Engagement rather than confrontation could alter Syria's strategic orientation over time, the reasoning went, ending what was believed to be an 'alliance of convenience' with Iran.

The Syrian uprising erupted as the West was coming to terms with its diminished military clout, made clear by NATO's Libya operation. Although ultimately successful, this had demonstrated serious European military deficiencies and a marked dependency on American logistics and muscle. There was no appetite among European generals and NATO leaders for what would be a significantly larger military operation in Syria, which would certainly require US backing that was unlikely to be forthcoming. Indeed, the Obama administration seemed inclined to reduce US involvement in the Middle East so as to focus on other global priorities.

As important was the fact that, by the time the Syrian uprising had gathered enough momentum and media visibility, initial Western optimism about the Arab uprisings was already evaporating. Difficult transitions in Egypt and Tunisia, the cost and chaos of Libya and the rise of political Islamism were stark reminders of how the Arab revolutions could produce outcomes at odds with Western interests. This was compounded by a general Western weariness about involvement in the Middle East after the unhappy Western adventures in Afghanistan and Iraq. A view that Arabs were ungrateful, incoherent and inconsistent in their relations with the West had settled among average citizens and officials. Clinton's tumultuous reception in Cairo in March 2011 reflected the widespread scepticism among revolutionary activists about US policy. This revived the debate about the desirability of political liberalisation in the Arab world over the perceived certainty of secular authoritarianism. With Syria in particular, its revolution came later, was more violent, had a stronger Islamist colour and looked less telegenic than the others, and so attracted noticeably less sympathy from general Western public opinion. Polling in the US showed considerable opposition to arming the rebels or direct intervention.[26]

There were other, Syria-specific, reasons for Western reluctance. Firstly, the geopolitical costs were seen to outweigh the merits of forceful intervention. Staunch Russian and Chinese opposition to any UN-sanctioned intervention in Syria raised concerns about renewed disagreement and bad blood. The episode of Libya had left lasting bruises, as both China and Russia claimed that NATO countries had used a UN mandate to 'protect civilians' to promote a regime-change agenda. As states whose political systems and records do not accord with Western practices, China and Russia were keen to prevent the external imposition of norms and rules that could eventually affect them.

Conversely, some Syrians viewed Russian and Chinese obstruction as useful to Western states as it concealed their own indecisiveness and averseness. Western officials were, however, pessimistic about their ability to win over Russia and China, while the costs of circumventing the UNSC were judged to be too high, given the parallels with the 2003 invasion of Iraq, the low regional standing of Western states and other potential legal complications. Relations with Russia were already deteriorating, ahead of Vladimir Putin's return to the Kremlin. Syria was just one issue among a complex set of disputes that include Eastern Europe, Georgia, energy, missile defence, Russia's domestic policies and the need to maintain pressure (along with China) on Iran and North Korea.

This deadlock was compounded by foot-dragging from leading democratic nations of the developing world to mobilise against the Assad regime. This was principally the case with Brazil, South Africa and India: the first two sat until late 2011 on the UNSC and the latter until late 2012. The opposition of much of the developing world to UN sanctions on Syria, let alone intervention, foreboded costly diplomacy for the West. India in particular mounted a principled opposition against any such action, seeing the crisis through similar lenses as Russia (mainly non-interference and the rise of Islamism) but also through aversion to perceived neo-colonial ambitions.

Secondly, Syria's complex terrain and the ability of Western states to navigate it, and so keep up with the conflict's evolution, emerged as impediments to action. The heterogeneous make-up and geographical distribution of Syrian society, not-well-understood historical and political grievances and the proximity of troubled countries guaranteed that intervention would be costly. Parallels with the Balkans as well as nearby Lebanon and Iraq saturated the Western debate and fuelled concerns about entanglement in an intractable conflict. Western governments doubted both the ability of Jordan and Turkey to host and facilitate a massive covert operation and the staying power of the Gulf states.

Thirdly, the opportunity to erode the Levantine reach of Iran, portrayed in the West as the top geopolitical threat, was tempered by the concern that greater chaos could ensue. An intervention in Syria could derail Western diplomatic efforts to jump-start already uncertain talks with Tehran, and would run the risk of precipitating a regional escalation. It would also put additional demands on US and European military capabilities, complicating potential military options against Iran.

A related concern here was the impact on Israel. Its conservative, Iran-focused defence establishment proved unwilling at first to trade certainty with Assad for unknown outcomes that would change the strategic landscape on its northern border, including with Hizbullah. As a result, Israeli anxiety about changes in Syria became a key factor in Western calculations.

Fourthly, the anticipation that the Syrian crisis, and ensuing power and security vacuum, would rekindle the fortunes of Salafi-jihadi ideologies and actors pervaded Western thinking. The fear was that once again the West would, in effect, ally with and empower radical Islamists with a profoundly anti-Western outlook, thus helping them establish a presence close to Europe and the Mediterranean. The perception that the uprising was primarily Sunni and Islamist in nature also concerned those in the West who cared about the fate of secularism and minorities, especially Christians. Some Western intelligence officials even reminisced about their cooperation with Syrian security agencies against al-Qaeda and other jihadi operatives. A related concern was that Western jihadis would join the ranks of the insurgency and, on returning to their home country, pose an internal domestic threat.

Together, these concerns have led to Western hesitancy, in particular from the US. As a result, governments have had to fight the perception among Syrian opposition leaders that their policy paralysis amounted to de facto acceptance of the Assad regime, and that their conviction over the inevitability of Assad's demise served as a pretext for minimal involvement.

Russia takes a stand

The firm Russian stance over Syria has proved to be a key factor in the survival of the Assad regime. Relations between the two countries, dating back to the 1950s, suffered from the collapse of the Soviet Union when Syria, deprived of its financial and military patron, had to adapt to American hegemony in the Middle East in the 1990s. The increasingly assertive tone of Russian foreign policy from the third term of Vladimir Putin, the failure of the peace process and the more aggressive Middle East policy of the Bush administration, including the 2003 invasion of Iraq, drove the two countries closer again, although not to the point that Russia considered Syria a vital ally.

Moscow's reasoning over the Syrian conflict is manifold. Its foremost motivation is to firmly defend the international legal principle of non-interference in the internal affairs of sovereign states and the role of the UNSC, where it holds veto power, in authorising military intervention. Russia sees these principles as cornerstones of a fair international order that is coming under relentless Western assault. After a decade of weakness and decline, Russia's rationale extends to the issue of national pride and global standing: its success in protecting Assad or brokering a political transition that preserves its interests in Syria amounts to a test of its credibility in the Arab world and beyond.

This world view is aggravated by a fundamental distrust of US global motivations, as Moscow sees Western policy as trying to shape and benefit strategically from the Arab revolutions. Indeed Moscow views the Syrian uprising in the context of the Western-backed colour revolutions that toppled autocratic governments in its immediate neighbourhood. Russia also resented the way Western states interpreted UNSC Resolution 1973 to support Libyan rebels and bring down the Gadhafi regime. Russian diplomats felt misled and manipulated after they agreed to the Libya resolution, and this bitter experience has informed their position regarding Syria. It has also fed Moscow's fear that the

West could use such precedents to intervene in the territories of the former Soviet Union, including Russia itself.

Moscow has taken a cynical view of the transformations in the Arab world, seeing disruptive rather than democratic forces at work. It sees these changes as fraught with danger to the regional order and calculates that they will undermine the strength of the Arab states. It has read the Syrian uprising as a militant Islamist challenge against state authority that should legitimately be confronted by all means, as Russia is doing in the North Caucasus.

Moscow considers the Western embrace of the Arab revolutions as immature and misguided, demonstrating naïveté about the risks posed by Islamist movements. Moscow has struggled to contain Islamist insurgencies in the Caucasus and associated terrorism that reached the large cities of European Russia. In the 1990s, the security elite perceived that Russia's territorial integrity was under threat; those fears have not entirely receded. The notion that Islamist gains in the Arab world would inevitably inspire an Islamist renewal in the Caucasus is entrenched. The geographical proximity of Syria has amplified the concern that Chechen, Caucasian and Salafi fighters would find a nearby battleground and haven. Unsurprisingly, therefore, Russia quickly embraced the narrative pushed by the Assad regime that the uprising was the doing of Islamist and foreign fighters. Its media highlighted the presence of foreign fighters early on, frequently and in an exaggerated manner before it became a serious issue.

Its Middle Eastern interests have also informed Russian policy. The downfall of the Gadhafi regime deprived it of one of its last Arab allies, thus increasing the relative importance of Assad. Russia's strategic ties with Iran are bound up with the Syrian issue, because Tehran is Assad's closest ally. Russian credibility and regional standing would gravely suffer should Assad fall.

Contentious relations with the Gulf states have also shaped Moscow's response. The former are allies of the West with an antagonistic history towards communism and see Russia as a prime enabler and protector of Iranian ambitions. Moscow has long suspected the Gulf states of funding and harbouring Islamist militants who fought in the Caucasus, and resents the role of Saudi Arabia in propagating Wahhabi ideology and of Qatar in providing media exposure to militant groups. Minimal economic and cultural relations compound already weak and strained relations.

Russia's long relationship with Syria means that it has specific interests to preserve there. Russia stands to lose considerably should Assad fall, as a new government may well turn its back on it, cancelling previous agreements. Russia currently enjoys the use of a naval facility in Tartous, its sole base of this nature outside the former Soviet Union, which allows the Russian navy to sustain a presence in the Mediterranean. Their long military relationship, embodied by several hundred Russian military personnel on Syrian soil, extends to arms sales as well. After Russia wrote off Syria's considerable debt of US$10bn in 2005, it once again became Syria's top arms supplier. Syria was Russia's second-largest weapons export market in 2011, totalling around US$500m, where Syrian procurement included air defence systems, anti-ship missiles and helicopters.[27] This is an important issue for the Russian defence industry, but one that may well not survive regime change in Syria.

Another, often overlooked dimension of Syrian-Russian ties are the communities of Syrians with links to Russia. Between 10,000 and 40,000 Russian nationals live in Syria, the result of decades of human and cultural exchanges.[28] Ethnic Circassians, who moved to the Levant in the nineteenth century, have often allied with the Assad regime, as has Syria's large Armenian community. Religious solidarity also matters. Most Christians in Syria belong to the Orthodox Church, which supports the

Assad regime because of the religious freedoms it allows and the economic benefits it derives from this alliance. As the modern Russian state embraced its Orthodox identity, it also assumed abroad, in the eyes of Orthodox communities, the role of a quasi-protector. The fate of these communities and the need to relocate them in case of large-scale retribution would place a significant burden onto Russia.

The different layers of its ties to Syria mean that Russia has been keen to promote a negotiated political solution, even as it has refused the resignation of Assad as a precondition to talks. After initially denouncing important Syrian opposition groups as illegitimate, Moscow called for national reconciliation between all parties (including Assad). It has engaged the whole range of Syrian opposition groups (including the SNC and, more frequently, more accommodationist groups like the NCC), but signalled no willingness to shift on the fundamental question of Assad's fate. Putin explained Russia's goals as follows: 'We must do as much as possible to force the conflicting sides to reach a peaceful political solution to all contentious questions … We must strive to promote such a dialogue. Of course, this work is much more complex and subtle than intervening by brute force, but only this can provide a long-term settlement and further stable development of the region and of the Syrian state.'[29]

Russia may be willing to facilitate the departure of Assad if its interests in the country are preserved and provided it did not involve any departure from the principles that Moscow has espoused at the UNSC. A bargaining process has yet to start, and the price Moscow would want to extract from it remains unknown, but Russia could use the perception of its presumed leverage over the Syrian military elite, which trained in Soviet then Russian schools, to emerge as a key mediator in any Syrian transition.

In the meantime, the Russian strategy has been to contain the Syrian crisis within the UN, highlight the lack of Western political vision, play up the Islamist and jihadi character of the rebellion and emphasise the hypocrisy of the Gulf states and Turkey in hosting, funding and arming the opposition. Thanks to its veto on the UNSC, and in association with China, Russia has defeated three draft resolutions to shield the Assad regime from international wrath. The first veto was exercised in October 2011 against a draft resolution under Chapter 41 threatening sanctions against the Syrian government. The second was in February 2012, to prevent a draft resolution that condemned violence but, according to Russia, placed disproportionate responsibility and blame on the Assad regime. The third was in June of that year in opposition to a draft, led by Annan in Geneva, that required Damascus to abide by previous resolutions calling for an end to violence. Moscow saw this as potentially allowing coercive measures and even military action against Damascus. Embarrassingly for Moscow, the spike in government-inflicted violence after each veto was widely interpreted as the result of a Russian green light.

Despite its resistance on the international stage, Moscow needed to demonstrate its seriousness about the political track, by continuously engaging Annan and Brahimi and agreeing to the Geneva transitional plan. At times Russia also expressed displeasure with Assad and pressured him to accept the Arab League and UN initiatives. After Syria ultimately rejected it, Russia (and China) abstained in a UN General Assembly vote that condemned the violence by an overwhelming majority. It framed its position as wanting to avoid state failure in Syria and further destabilisation of the Middle East. Putin said Russia was 'not concerned with the fate of Assad's regime' and, breaking with Russia's interpretation of the uprising, admitted that 'undoubtedly there is a call for change [in Syria]'.[30]

Nonetheless, Russia has continued to supply the Syrian military with weaponry and ammunition, including refurbished helicopters and other high-tech systems. Faced with international outrage, Moscow protested that these deliveries were part of existing military contracts it would honour. Lavrov further claimed that: 'We are not delivering offensive weapons to Syria. We are not delivering weapons which could be used in a civil war.'[31] In late 2012, reports surfaced that Russia had printed and transferred 240 tonnes of new Syrian money.[32] Russian material support has become crucial to the Assad regime's viability as its resources shrink. Russian motivations in providing such a lifeline are complex and double-edged: it provides leverage and access, and buttresses its credibility as a partner, but antagonises the Syrian opposition and much of the Arab world.

By late 2012, however, Russian assessments about Assad's prospects had considerably dimmed. Deputy Foreign Minister Mikhail Bogdanov told a parliamentary committee: 'Unfortunately, it is impossible to exclude a victory of the Syrian opposition ... We must look squarely at the facts, and the trend now suggests that the regime and the government in Syria are losing more and more control and more and more territory.'[33]

Military constraints to intervention

As the debate over intervention intensified, Syria's military capabilities became a central concern for NATO, US and European defence planners. The size, equipment, organisation and battle-readiness of the Syrian military posed a greater challenge than its Libyan counterpart ever could.

The Syrian military was built to wage potential inter-state wars. The country has maintained contentious relations with militarily stronger neighbours: Iraq under Saddam Hussein, US-backed and nuclear-armed Israel, and NATO member Turkey. It has also faced weak polities, including divided Lebanon, fragile Jordan, stateless and militant Palestinians, and post-Saddam Iraq. The continued state of war with Israel over the Israeli-occupied Golan Heights provided another reason to justify high defence spending. It was also the result of the military background and ethos of Hafez al-Assad and other Syrian leaders, the army's role as an instrument of empowerment of Alawites, and other minorities, and Syria's self-image as the protector of Arabism.

Syria's quest for external security and regional reach needed to surmount considerable structural constraints and acute resource scarcity. Syria's economy, industrial base and relatively small energy endowment could not sustain its military ambitions. It, therefore, depended on foreign patronage and rent, as well as on asymmetric strategies, including the development of proxies in neighbouring states as an instrument of influence, deterrence and action. However, the loss of the Soviet Union as a foreign patron, limited financial resources, antiquated military doctrine and organisation, limited human talent, and a small indigenous defence industry further impeded Syria's ambitions. A renewed effort to modernise and upgrade Syria's defences, especially its air defences, started in the mid-2000s. By 2011, the Syrian military was a diminished force, but one still able to inflict serious damage on potential attackers.

Regime security was a key objective of the security sector, which was organised to guard the regime against potential external and domestic threats, and to do so without itself posing a threat to the regime. Ensuring loyalty superseded the maximisation of military performance, which meant allocating resources to build loyal, albeit competing, security agencies able to protect the regime but not grow to the point where they could pose a challenge. This led to the multiplication of security agencies, a politicised system that managed them and the preferential allocation of resources to units deemed more loyal.

An additional consideration for defence planners would be the fate of the Syrian army, post-intervention. Most scenarios would necessitate at least its incapacitation, which would require the mobilisation of significant Western military assets over a sustained period of time. The size of such a military undertaking was made clear by the Chairman of the US Joint Chiefs of Staff General Martin Dempsey: 'If you chose to establish [a safe zone/ no-fly zone inside Syria] you would assume the responsibility for protecting it. If you are tasked to protect it you have to look at those who might seek to attack it or to influence it and that could take you, depending on weapons systems, it could take you to a limited no-fly zone [and] it could take you to the point of having to interdict air and ballistic missile systems.'[34] Dempsey further ridiculed the often-made comparison with the Libya operation, saying it was a source of 'amusement'.[35]

Defence planners have derived a lesson from the Iraq war: that a country's military is needed to restore security and ensure the functioning of institutions during volatile transition periods. Syria's significant chemical weapons arsenal and porous borders strengthened that working assumption. A standing Syrian military, it was believed in Western capitals, would be essential to secure both and undertake important security tasks, since no invasion force was being considered and a UN stabilisation force was unlikely. Therefore, any intervention would need to be calibrated not only to encourage more defections and shifts in loyalty but also to preserve the regular military and its chain of command, as much as possible.

Syria's geography emerged as another complicating factor. Along its 822km-long border lie Jordan and NATO member Turkey, where the US enjoys the use of military bases, both of which would provide an adequate staging ground. However, significant constituencies opposed to intervention in countries around Syria, Jordan and Turkey's own political considerations, as well as wider concerns about the regional impact, constrained military planning. In particular, the consensus on sheltering Lebanon from the Syrian crisis would be a major challenge.

Moreover, the geography of the fighting inside Syria amounted to a formidable obstacle that would be difficult to assess with certainty. This comprised the varied physical terrain, the deployment of forces, the growing urban character of the warfare, the presence of civilian combatants on all sides, the absence of a clear frontline and the associated difficulty of identifying friend from foe.

Chemical weapons: a red line?

Syria's large arsenal of chemical weapons poses a significant challenge.[36] Primarily developed to achieve strategic parity with Israel, the chemical weapons programme, whose existence Syria denies despite not being a signatory to the Chemical Weapons Convention, includes unknown quantities of sarin, VX and mustard gas. These nerve agents can be weaponised into artillery shells, chemical bombs and missiles. Laboratories, production facilities and storage spaces are located across the country, including in areas close to the fighting. In July 2012, a foreign ministry spokesman, trying to dispel fears about use of chemical weapons against civilians, inadvertently acknowledged the existence of these stocks. Explaining that such weapons would only be used against 'external aggression', he added, 'all varieties of these weapons are stored and secured by the Syrian armed forces and under [their] direct supervision'.[37]

Concerns related to chemical weapons were manifold: use against civilians or enemies; transfer to an ally, especially a non-state actor like Hizbullah; loss to groups with a radical agenda, including al-Qaeda affiliates; possible transfer to a consolidated Alawite area; loss of expertise and materials. Israel in particular was worried about such possibilities, especially as reports circulated that Hizbullah units operated in the vicinity of sensitive facilities.[38]

It remains uncertain whether the regime would use such weapons. Their military effectiveness is doubtful and dispersion highly problematic. At the same time, the psychological impact of such weapons could terrorise populations and rebels, while the extremely difficult task of investigating and attributing responsibility for a chemical attack could afford Assad enough deniability and ambiguity to test international resolve. The threat of chemical weapons is a double-edged sword for him: while it serves as a reminder of his nuisance capacity and a tool of coercion, it could also force the international community to overcome its reluctance to intervene. In November 2012, Western intelligence acquired information that showed Syrian forces were readying chemical agents, possibly to be loaded onto airborne bombs. Concerted pressure through several channels, including Russia, forced Assad to reverse course.[39] In a separate incident the next month, unconfirmed reports emerged that the Syrian regime had used non-lethal chemical weapons in Homs.[40]

Tellingly, the only explicit red line drawn by Western countries was over the chemical weapons. In August 2012, Obama stated publicly that: 'We have been very clear to the Assad regime, but also to other players on the ground, that a red line for us is we start seeing a whole bunch of chemical weapons moving around or being utilised. That would change my calculus.'[41] In later months, however, the changing US position on what action would constitute a violation of this red line, how to attribute responsibility and how to respond appropriately reflected the difficulty of calibrating a proper signal. Dempsey confessed that: 'The act of preventing the use of chemical weapons would be almost unachievable.'[42] Obama warned of 'consequences' should chemical weapons be used rather than stressing prevention as a goal, while Clinton warned that the US would 'certainly [plan] to take action' should there be 'credible evidence that the Assad regime has resorted to using chemical weapons against their own people'.[43] The size of the challenge certainly affected US calculations as direct military action to secure or destroy chemical storage facilities, through air and missile strikes, would be incredibly complicated. US intelligence assessed that securing chemical weapons facilities would require as many as 75,000 troops.[44] To monitor and possibly secure these capabilities, the US sent advanced teams to Jordan and Turkey. At the same time, whether and how the US would respond in case of a suspected or established use of chemical weapons became a test of US credibility, because of international norms against use of weapons of mass destruction.

The Western debate over assisting the rebellion

As the death toll has increased and the regime has deployed its entire conventional military arsenal, the Western debate over intervention has intensified. With ground intervention dismissed early on by every country as too risky and costly (except in case of use or transfer of chemical weapons and in case of cross-border hostilities), options considered have included no-fly zones and safe zones. Proponents and critics have debated the lessons of humanitarian precedents in Iraq and the Balkans in the 1990s. Safe zones, which had a dubious record in Bosnia, require significant ground presence and a strong mandate. No-fly zones would entail a massive military operation to disable Syria's sizeable air-defence capabilities.

The argument in favour of direct and forceful intervention held that the failure to do so would allow for a protracted, more destructive and more destabilising conflict. As it continued to escalate, more moderate elements of the Syrian rebellion would be deprived of crucial backing, while more radical groups could tap into stable sources of support from the Gulf. The ensuing risk was that Western states may eventually be dragged into a more complex conflict in case of sectarian cleansing or WMD use, without reliable local partners. Thus, a failure to act would cause the very radicalisation, state collapse and regional fallout feared by Western states, and also create space for jihadi groups to operate in the heart of the Levant. The costs of containing the conflict, brokering a political solution and rebuilding the Syrian state would also be greater.

Syrian oppositionists were, however, divided over intervention. A sizeable segment disapproved on principle of any Western action, fearing it would undermine and taint their struggle and precipitate civil war. Others argued that given the regime's escalation and the imbalance of power, foreign intervention was required. By late 2011, armed rebels started demanding an internationally imposed no-fly zone over northern parts of Syria, ostensibly to protect civilians. At the time, the humanitarian rationale appeared weak as the Syrian military made no use of its air force, instead relying mostly on artillery and ground operations. Rebel commanders admitted to other motivations. A no-fly zone would signal Western seriousness, thus encouraging the defection of senior regime figures and officers, seen to be still hedging. It would also allow for the defection of mechanised and armoured units, more visible and more vulnerable from the air, and it would help rebels capture and occupy barracks, government buildings, roads and other infrastructure.

Assad's resort to air power, repeated massacres of civilians and the influx of refugees into neighbouring countries, starting in the spring of 2012, strengthened the case for no-fly zones and safe havens along the Turkish and Jordanian borders. Turkey especially advocated this option after several cross-border incidents over the summer, including shelling and the downing of a Turkish jet which had flown into Syrian airspace. The possibility of imposing a de facto no-fly zone by deploying *Patriot* missile batteries and surface-to-air missiles along the Syrian-Turkish border was raised, but discord within NATO hindered any such plans. (A strictly defensive deployment was, nonetheless, put in place, in early 2013, after a Turkish request.)

Arming or not arming?
With the option of no-fly and safe zones discarded, the debate among Western governments shifted to whether and how to

assist the Syrian armed opposition. There were clear arguments in favour of training and targeted provision of weaponry to the rebels: it would provide the West with partners within the armed opposition; it would help organise and moderate rebel factions; it would help create viable alternatives to the increasingly prominent jihadi groups; and it would displace smuggling and other networks. Militarisation of the opposition had become an inevitable and irreversible trend of the Syrian revolution, and this reality needed to be engaged with and managed. Otherwise, rebels would develop their own supply routes and become either self-reliant or dependent on foreign and local actors with radical, destabilising or uncompromising agendas. Creating rebel dependency on Western-friendly political actors was seen as essential to preserving the unity of Syria, preventing warlordism, containing jihadism, and designing inclusive political mechanisms.

Moreover, proponents of targeted provision of weaponry argued that, if channelled through the political opposition, such assistance would empower the latter and help promote its dominance over military commanders. This would create conditions conducive to a political settlement and an inclusive governance of liberated territories. As the Assad regime's military superiority was seen as a main reason for its unwillingness to negotiate a power transition, a military stalemate or a decisive shift on the ground was believed to be needed to jump-start genuine political talks.

The US administration, which had committed to the Geneva plan, worried that direct provision of weaponry would undercut a diplomatic solution and would have a thin legal basis, in the absence of UN or NATO cover. Critics of the administration asserted that the US and Russia were engaged in a cynical dance: the US overstated Russian influence in Syria and hid behind Russian obstruction to conceal its own indecision and lack of strategy, while Russia engaged in the motions of diplomacy despite having neither the intention nor the leverage to sideline Assad.

The blowback of a venture with similarities to Afghanistan in the 1980s and the legacy of the decade-long 'war on terror' weighed heavily on the deliberations of the US administration. The emergence in late 2011 of jihadi groups that conducted suicide attacks, car bombings and military operations bolstered these concerns, especially when JN, the most prominent jihadi group operating in Syria, was identified in late 2012 by the US as an affiliate of AQI and listed as a foreign terrorist organisation.

Furthermore, there was much concern among US officials that providing weapons would not translate into leverage, or even moderate rebel factions, and that they would inevitably fall into the hands of radical groups. The dysfunction and disorganisation of the Syrian armed opposition compounded this fear. Since its inception, the nominal leadership of the FSA had failed to impose command-and-control over affiliated units. This was due as much to the meagre resources available to its top command-ers as to competition among them, lack of·political leadership and the quick transformation of the uprising. By mid-2012, only half of all rebel groups claimed membership in the FSA, while many of the largest brigades (Farouq and Tawheed) operated autonomously. The rise of jihadist factions, including JN, further validated US reluctance. Providing weaponry in such conditions, it was believed in Washington, would only increase the level of violence and exacerbate the moral as well as strategic entangle-ment of indirect intervention. It would also fail to decisively tip the military balance against the regime forces.

The modalities of targeted provision of weaponry required deep and direct US involvement, including the establishment of political and military criteria and the commitment of significant intelligence resources to identify and vet acceptable groups. It would also require coordination with Jordan, Turkey and the Gulf states. These countries were already providing support of this nature, but had differing agendas in Syria and didn't necessarily share US concerns about specific rebel groups or loss of weaponry. Another type of assistance that has been considered is intelligence-sharing, and there have been reports of this type of assistance for select rebel groups, but no sign of sustained intelligence coordination.

Finally, the US hesitated over the type and quality of the arms. Syrian rebels demanded access to weaponry to outmatch Assad's capabilities, including anti-tank weaponry and man-shouldered anti-aircraft missiles (MANPADs) to erode his air superiority. The fear that radical or jihadi groups would eventually seize such weaponry was shared by all states supporting the opposition. This included Turkey, which was concerned that separatist Kurdish militants may acquire them from Syrian rebels. Israel too was opposed to the provision of MANPADs for fear they would eventually erode Israel's own air superiority over its neighbours. As a result, the US pressured Gulf countries to deny rebels access to advanced weaponry.

In early 2013, the extent of division within the US administration over the matter of provision of weaponry surfaced. The CIA, backed by the Pentagon and the State Department, had developed plans in mid-2012 to vet and equip specific rebel groups, but the White House rejected these plans, on the grounds that they were too risky and would fail to make a decisive difference. This resistance was informed by complex geopolitics, concerns that such aid would only fuel the conflict and result in a blowback, questions about the legality and effectiveness of such assistance and the difficulty of designing proper mechanisms to deploy it.[45]

Instead, the Obama administration settled on providing significant humanitarian help to Syrians in need, inside and outside the country, and non-lethal assistance to select rebel groups operating under the FSA umbrella, primarily in the form of secure communications equipment, medical supplies and food, thus freeing rebel resources for other purposes. The US government has also invested significant resources and energy in training civilian activists, who it hopes will provide the backbone of local governance, and in post-war planning to help Syria's political and economic reconstruction (although these efforts are contingent upon internal dynamics that the US barely understands, let alone controls). In December 2011, it allowed the establishment of an NGO, the Syrian Support Group, to raise funds for rebel groups operating under the Provincial Military Councils of the FSA. This compromise failed, however, to convince Syrian rebels, who started complaining vocally about anaemic Western help in the summer of 2012.

The US stance over weapons deliveries contrasts with the more forthcoming position of France and the UK. Both have shown an interest in lifting the arms embargo, adopted by the EU in 2011, and have been politically more supportive of the Syrian opposition groups, pushing for greater assistance as well as the establishment of a transitional government. However, the reluctance of more risk-averse EU countries, such as Germany and Sweden who are more in sync with the US position, has prevented French and UK efforts to up military support for rebels.

Notes

1   David Ignatius, 'The Arab revolution grows up', *The Washington Post*, 2 February 2011, http://www.washingtonpost.com/wp-dyn/content/article/2011/02/01/AR2011020106351.html.

2   Haddad, 'Why Syria is unlikely to be next... for now', *Arab Reform Bulletin*, 9 March 2011, http://carnegieendowment.org/2011/03/09/why-syria-is-unlikely-to-be-next-.-.-.-for-now/6bhl; and Michael Broning, 'The sturdy house Assad built',

Foreign Affairs, 7 March 2011, http://www.foreignaffairs.com/articles/67561/michael-broening/the-sturdy-house-that-assad-built.

3   Interview with European diplomat, Damascus, May 2011.

4   For more on the EU-Syria relationship, see: Michael Elleman, Dina Esfandiary and Emile Hokayem, 'Syria's Proliferation Challenge and the European Union's Response', Non-Proliferation Paper,

no. 20, July 2012, http://www.sipri.org/research/disarmament/eu-consortium/publications/Nonproliferationpaper-20.

5   Elleman, Esfandiary and Hokayem, 'Syria's Proliferation Challenge and the European Union's Response'.

6   'Senator John Kerry on U.S. Policy Toward the Middle East', Carnegie Endowment for International Peace, 16 March 2011, http://www.carnegieendowment.org/2011/03/16/senator-john-kerry-on-u.s.-policy-toward-middle-east/1fd.

7   Dina Hughes, 'As Syria Conflict Rages On, Clinton's Rhetoric Intensifies', *ABC News*, 13 June 2012, http://abcnews.go.com/Politics/syria-conflict-rages-clintons-rhetoric-intensifies/story?id=16561069#.UIvKJY6CgWk.

8   Nicole Gaouette, 'Clinton says US won't intervene in Syria, sees progress in Libya fight', *Bloomberg News*, 28 March 2011, http://www.bloomberg.com/news/2011-03-27/u-s-won-t-intervene-in-syria-unrest-clinton-says-on-cbs.html.

9   'Secretary Clinton meets with EU High Representative Ashton', U.S. Department of State Official Blog, 17 May 2011, http://blogs.state.gov/index.php/site/entry/clinton_ashton_syria_libya.

10 'Obama's Speech on U.S. Policies in Middle East and North Africa', Office of the Press Secretary, The White House, 19 May 2011, http://iipdigital.usembassy.gov/st/english/texttrans/2011/05/20110519124857su0.5616201.html#ixzz2Rx6bEeAB.

11 'Al-safir al-amriki: Biladi tad'am hiwaran bayna al-mu'rida al-suriyya w-al-nizam li-inha' al-azma', *al-Arabiya*, 21 June 2011, http://www.alarabiya.net/articles/2011/06/21/154269.html.

12 Macon Phillips, 'President Obama: "The future of Syria must be determined by its people, but President Bashar al-Assad is standing in their way"', *The White House Blog*, 18 August 2011, http://www.whitehouse.gov/blog/2011/08/18/president-obama-future-syria-must-be-determined-its-people-president-bashar-al-assad.

13 'Confronting Damascus: U.S. Policy Toward the Evolving Situation in Syria', testimony given to this hearing at the U.S. House Foreign Affairs Subcommittee on the Middle East and South Asia, 14 December 2011.

14 Mohamed Fadel Fahmy, 'Arab League calls for unity government in Syria', *CNN.com*, 23 January 2012, http://edition.cnn.com/2012/01/22/world/meast/syria-unrest.

15 'General Assembly Adopts Resolution Strongly Condemning "Widespread and Systematic" Human Rights Violations by Syrian Authorities', UN Department of Public Information, 16 February 2012, http://www.un.org/News/Press/docs/2012/ga11207.doc.htm.

16 'Action Group for Syria: Final Communiqué', UN Action Group for Syria, 30 June 2012, http://www.un.org/News/dh/infocus/Syria/FinalCommuniqueActionGroupforSyria.pdf.

17 Kofi Annan, 'My departing advice on how to save Syria', *Financial Times*, 2 August 2012, http://www.ft.com/cms/s/2/b00b6ed4-dbc9-11e1-8d78-00144feab49a.html.

18 Henry Meyer, 'UN Envoy Warns of Syria "Hell" as Beheaded Bodies Found', Bloomberg News, 31 December 2012, http://www.

bloomberg.com/news/2012-12-30/syrian-forces-retake-town-as-un-s-brahimi-warns-of-hell-.html.

19 Ellen Barry, 'Insisting on Assad's Exit Will Cost More Lives, Russian Says', *The New York Times*, 29 December 2012, http://www.nytimes.com/2012/12/30/world/middleeast/syria.html?_r=0.

20 'Humanitarian Intervention in Syria: The Legal Basis', Public International Law & Policy Group, July 2012, http://publicinternationallawandpolicygroup.org/wp-content/uploads/2012/08/PILPG-The-Legal-Basis-for-Humanitarian-Intervention-in-Syria.pdf.

21 Paragraphs 138 and 139 of the 2005 World Summit Outcome, adopted 15 September 2005 by the United Nations General Assembly. Full text available: http://responsibilitytoprotect.org/world%20summit%20outcome%20doc%202005%281%29.pdf.

22 'Data suggests Syria death toll could be more than 60,000, says UN human rights office', UN News Centre, 2 January 2013, http://www.un.org/apps/news/story.asp?NewsID=43866#.USIOdfImTtg.

23 See the 'Regional Overview' from the UNHCR's Inter-agency Information Sharing Portal: http://data.unhcr.org/syrianrefugees/regional.php.

24 '2012 UNHCR country operations profile – Syrian Arab Republic', http://www.unhcr.org/pages/49e486a76.html.

25 Stephanie Nebehay, 'Most Houla victims killed in summary executions: U.N.', Reuters, 29 May 2012, http://www.reuters.com/article/2012/05/29/us-syria-un-idUSBRE84S10020120529.

26 Telhami and Steven Kull, 'Americans on the Middle East: A Study of American Public Opinion', Program on International Policy Attitudes, 8 October 2012, http://sadat.umd.edu/MiddleEast_Oct12_rpt.pdf.

27 Andrew Kramer, 'Russia Sending Missile Systems to Shield Syria', *The New York Times*, 15 June 2012, http://www.nytimes.com/2012/06/16/world/europe/russia-sending-air-and-sea-defenses-to-syria.html.

28 'Russia's Syrian stance: principled self-interest', IISS *Strategic Comments*, vol. 18, no. 31, September 2012, http://www.iiss.org/en/publications/strategic%20comments/sections/2012-bb59/russias-syrian-stance--principled-self-interest-3743.

29 Dalal Mawad and Rick Gladstone, 'Russia Prods Syria's President Assad With Message of Growing Impatience', *The New York Times*, 9 July 2012, http://www.nytimes.com/2012/07/10/world/middleeast/bashar-al-assad-meets-with-kofi-annan.html.

30 Barry, 'Insisting on Assad's Exit Will Cost More Lives, Russian Says'.

31 'Lavrov Denies Russian Arms Supplies to Syria', *Rian Novosti*, 29 December 2012, http://en.rian.ru/politics/20121229/178479802.html.

32 Dafna Linzer, Michael Grabell and Jeff Larson, 'Flight Records Say Russia Sent Syria Tons of Cash', *ProPublica*, 26 November 2012, http://www.propublica.org/article/flight-records-list-russia-sending-tons-of-cash-to-syria.

33 Barry, 'Russia Offers a Dark View of Assad's Chances for Survival', *The New York Times*, 13 December 2012, http://www.nytimes.com/2012/12/14/world/

middleeast/russian-envoy-says-syrian-leader-is-losing-control.html?pagewanted=all.

[34] Kim Sengupta, 'America's most senior general warns against rash action on Syria and Iran', *The Independent,* 31 August 2012, http://www.independent.co.uk/news/world/americas/americas-most-senior-general-warns-against-rash-actionon-syria-and-iran-8096881.html.

[35] *Ibid.*

[36] Syria conducted research to develop biological weapons but they are not believed to be easily deployable. Its covert nuclear programme was destroyed in an Israeli air-strike in 2007. The fate of up to 50 tonnes of unenriched uranium believed to be in Syria's possession is unknown.

[37] 'Unease grows over Syria's chemical weapons', *IISS Strategic Comments,* vol. 18, no. 25, August 2012, http://www.iiss.org/en/publications/strategic%20comments/sections/2012-bb59/unease-grows-over-syrias-chemical-weapons-4510.

[38] David E. Sanger and Eric Schmiit, 'Pentagon Says 75,000 Troops Might Be Needed to Seize Chemical Arms', *The New York Times,* 15 November 2012, http://www.nytimes.com/2012/11/16/world/middleeast/pentagon-sees-seizing-syria-chemical-arms-as-vast-task.html?pagewanted=all.

[39] Schmitt and Sanger, 'Hints of Syrian Chemical Push Set Off Global Effort to Stop It', *The New York Times,* 7 January 2013, http://www.nytimes.com/2013/01/08/world/middleeast/chemical-weapons-showdown-with-syria-led-to-rare-accord.html?pagewanted=all&_r=0.

[40] Josh Rogin, 'Exclusive: Secret State Department Cable: Chemical Weapons Used in Syria', *Foreign Policy,* 15 January 2013, http://thecable.foreignpolicy.com/posts/2013/01/15/secret_state_department_cable_chemical_weapons_used_in_syria.

[41] Mark Landler, 'Obama Threatens Force Against Syria', *The New York Times,* 20 August 2012, http://www.nytimes.com/2012/08/21/world/middleeast/obama-threatens-force-against-syria.html.

[42] Spencer Ackerman and Noah Shachtman, 'Top U.S. General Says Stopping a Syrian Chemical Attack Is 'Almost Unachievable', *Wired,* 10 January 2013, http://www.wired.com/dangerroom/2013/01/syria-chem-military/.

[43] Peter Finn and Anne Gearan, 'Obama warns Syria amid rising concern over chemical weapons', *The Washington Post,* 3 December 2012, http://articles.washingtonpost.com/2012-12-03/world/35622995_1_nonessential-international-staff-chemical-weapons-assad-government.

[44] Sanger and Schmitt, 'Pentagon Says 75,000 Troops Might Be Needed to Seize Chemical Arms'.

[45] Michael Gordon and Landler, 'Backstage Glimpses of Clinton as Dogged Diplomat, Win or Lose', *The New York Times,* 2 February 2013, http://www.nytimes.com/2013/02/03/us/politics/in-behind-scene-blows-and-triumphs-sense-of-clinton-future.html.

As Syria descends into a multifaceted and intensifying civil war, any medium-term prognosis needs to consider the extent of political and sectarian factionalism, humanitarian dislocation, societal cohesion, state capability and foreign meddling. As of early 2013, however, reliable data and information about each of these factors remains sorely lacking, while political dynamics are fluid. Consequently, it is impossible to make a firm prediction about the situation in Syria, and where the conflict is heading. However, judging by the trajectory of each of these key drivers of conflict, Syria appears unlikely to recover its national unity and stability in the medium term. Direct violence has led to a massive death toll (around 70,000 by early 2013), a refugee crisis affecting one-fifth of the population and the destruction of entire residential neighbourhoods, all of which preclude quick stabilisation and reconstruction.

The country's physical continuity is interrupted by sieges (Homs, Aleppo, Deir Ez-Zor), and by checkpoints manned by Assad loyalists, rebels and a new class of criminals. As a result, highways are insecure, endangering travellers and the movement of goods. Syria's economy and overall development have been devastated: according to a comprehensive report by a

Syrian economic research centre, economic losses by the end of 2012 have been estimated at US$48.4bn; the cost of basic products has soared (the Consumer Price Index has increased by 51% in 18 months); and the official unemployment figure has tripled.[1]

Societal fragmentation

The very fabric of Syrian society is fraying under the weight of the conflict: belief in the nation-state and religious coexistence has weakened, individual and communal preservation have become paramount, and acts of violence – whether random or calculated – are easily rationalised.

While the struggle is not primarily defined by sectarianism, the warring sides increasingly brandish communal identity as a tool of protection, mobilisation and exclusion. Distrust among and within Syria's various social and confessional groups has deepened. Many Sunnis perceive themselves to be the victims of a repression approved, explicitly or tacitly, by many members of the main minority groups and designed to keep them away from power. As of late 2012, most casualties and refugees belonged to the Sunni community, and the physical devastation has primarily affected its residential neighbourhoods and villages. On the other hand, minorities observe with alarm and trepidation the growing radicalism of the opposition and its assumed hostility towards them. Jihadi violence and isolated instances of sectarian revenge have had a major psychological impact on minorities. Many Alawite families have abandoned large cities for the safety of their villages and joined regime-backed militias, while many Christians have begun making plans for expatriation to Lebanon and beyond. Shia communities have built closer ties with Hizbullah in Lebanon and Iraqi Shia parties, while the Kurds have looked to the Iraqi example of de facto autonomy.

Class divisions have also been amplified: fighters from mostly poor, rural backgrounds have spearheaded the battle in

Damascus and Aleppo, alienating urbanites in the process. Such divides can only sharpen as the struggle drags on. The pervasiveness of the violence and the rise of criminality have pushed many urban professionals into either leaving the country or retreating from public life; the poor working classes, who already had very little to lose, either carry most of the fighting or find themselves trapped and desperate.

The extent of the divisions that have ruptured during this conflict puts Syria's territorial integrity at stake. The imperative of communal retrenchment is powerful, and incentives exist for groups like the Alawites or the Kurds to carve out their own territories, even at great cost. Given the geographical distribution of Syria's different confessional groups, forced transfers of population or fear-driven voluntary displacement would be necessary to create homogenous areas. For example, half of the population of the nominally Alawite heartland is composed of members of Sunni and minority sects, complicated by the fact that many of them have long-standing familial and other ties with Alawites.

It is also important to bear in mind that there is no certainty that communities would remain united and cohesive, even in the face of perceived existential threats. Nearby examples show that intra-sectarian fragmentation is possible: during Lebanon's long civil war, while the Druze community remained largely unified, Christians split and supported competing leaders purporting to confront the same enemy. The prospects for the Alawite community to hold together should Damascus be lost or Assad be ousted are uncertain.

There are, however, forces that could help to hold Syria together, including its long-held, if currently battered, self-image as a key political and cultural actor in the Arab world. Despite the current rise in sectarianism, the country does have a tradition of religious moderation and coexistence, which could contribute to a more positive and cohesive dynamic. Local leaders around

Homs and Aleppo, for example, have often contained religious passions since the uprising began.

The condition of Syria's society at the time of the possible demise of Assad, in parallel with the extent of state collapse, would be a determining element of the country's future. The societal cost of the war and its rapidly rising humanitarian toll have created acute resentment that both compounds old grievances and creates new ones.

Who holds power?

Alongside the state of Syria's institutions and the cohesiveness of Syrian society, the domestic dispensation of power is the most crucial factor that will determine the nature and outcome of any transitional phase, whether negotiated or precipitated by events on the ground.

The key question for the medium term is who holds power in a fragmented Syria. The prospects are slim for a rapid and orderly collapse of the Assad regime replaced by a government with sufficient legitimacy and physical reach on the ground to govern effectively. The length and viciousness of the struggle over Syria has given rise to new local power-brokers and new allegiances that may well outlast the fall of the Assad regime.

Many leaders of the political opposition have seen their influence diminish as the struggle has expanded and distorted: busy with the politics of the opposition abroad but unable to deliver protection, assistance or governance, they have essentially become irrelevant to the dynamics of the struggle. The absence on the ground of officials from the SNC and the NC has hurt the standing of both. Therefore, the relative authority of the mainstream political opposition, itself fragmented, is diminishing as new rebel groups spring to the fore.

Across Syria new leaderships are emerging, deriving their authority from their provision of order and essential goods (food, medicine, etc.), but also through coercion and ideology. By early 2013, Syria's liberated regions were controlled by several hundred political and armed organisations, beset by rivalries. In towns and villages in Idlib, the north, the tribal east and neighbourhoods of Aleppo, the local administration has survived or has been taken over by revolutionary councils in the form of civil councils (*majalis*) and judicial courts (*mahakim*). In other areas, especially those close to heavy fighting, civilian combatants and armed factions have become the de facto rulers, expecting deference and preferential treatment, administering justice and regulating social life.

Though still bound by the common focus on fighting Assad and by certain operational requirements, inter-rebel tensions have developed. Few rebel forces operate nationally and the heavy cost paid by some has already fed expectations that their needs and political demands will be addressed before others.

Thus, in liberated areas, an uneasy balance exists between the various revolutionary factions, who enjoy varying degrees of local legitimacy and support. Councils established by local leaders, revolutionary activists or large rebel units so far lack the coherence and resources, let alone the political will, to coordinate and evolve into a proper, nationwide system of administration. Furthermore, some may not be able to sustain their power because of local pressure or their small size; large, better-resourced groups may supplant and absorb them. (The need for resources explains why, for example, a number of battalions in Idlib joined the Salafi-leaning Syrian Islamic Front to benefit from transfers of equipment from Ahrar Al-Sham and Suqoor Al-Sham.)

The military reality compounds opposition and rebel fragmentation, and administrative incoherence. Barring game-changing external developments, such as foreign-imposed safe zones, the rebellion cannot mount a decisive armed challenge unless it unifies and secures a sustained supply of quality weaponry. Without this, the regime's military superiority, however eroded, would allow it to continue to hold what it has defined as vital areas along the Damascus-Aleppo corridor and the northwest coastal areas. At the time of writing, much of the north and east is in insurgent hands but is exposed to air and missile attacks, while the areas south and east of Damascus have witnessed a rebel build-up since December 2012, suggesting a coming assault on Damascus. Rebel groups have so far demonstrated little ability to coordinate operationally and strategically across the various fronts: rebel commanders in the north have little information about what their counterparts around Damascus are planning. Deficient communications, lack of trust and differences in outlook and organisation explain this state of affairs. The SMC may be able to inject strategic and operational coherence, but this will require time and resources.

These facts on the ground have allowed new calculations and ambitions to come into play, ones that conflict with the goals, professed by much of the mainstream political opposition and revolutionary activists, of civilian authority and of a central and secular state. Indeed, Islamist groups have seen an opportunity to establish a state aligned with their own religious values, or at least to impose these on the territories they control – through, for example, the recourse to Muslim clerics as judges.[2] (One should also bear in mind that religious leaders are often a moderating force on combatants and do, in fact, reflect the more conservative nature of many Syrians in rural areas, rather than carry an extremist agenda.)

The transformation of these armed groups holds other dangers. Some have already engaged in criminal activities, including kidnappings, and other types of parasitic behaviour, such as levies on local businesses, to finance their operations, as happened in the border town of Azzaz. As the conflict lengthens, some may well fully transform into criminal gangs, and control over border points is already being contested, heightening the risks for neighbouring states.

Just as important are the Syrians who have turned their backs on the politics of revolution. The conflict has already driven away some of the most productive elements of Syrian society, who fled for their safety or out of despair and disgust. Many civilian activists who were central to the movement's origins have been alienated by its transformation into an armed uprising, while others have abandoned their initial ideals to fully embrace the rebellion. Faced with unpalatable choices, fence-sitting Syrians do not feel compelled to pick sides, prioritising survival over politics. All the while, many forms of peaceful dissent have remained alive: peaceful protests are still being held, revolutionary art and humour is thriving, newspapers have emerged in liberated areas and low-key dissent continues to occur in government agencies.

The Syrian state, which had already been weakened before the uprising, finds itself on the verge of collapse, as its legitimacy and its institutions, from the Ba'ath Party to the judiciary to its social agencies, crumble. Under Assad, its role was buttressed by a potent pan-Arab ideology that organised society, mobilised individuals despite their sub-national loyalties and justified the costs of authoritarian rule. The removal of this ideological glue, alongside growing inequalities and hardships, have decisively weakened the state and undermined its key ability to protect groups and individuals supporting Assad.

As a result, Assad's regime-cum-militia is losing the institutional tools needed for it to reinforce its war narrative: that it is a state fighting a criminal uprising. What is left of the state is, in fact, negligible, as the delivery of social services has been scaled back or totally abandoned in many regions and its administrative reach is undercut by shrinking resources and territorial losses to the rebels. As resources are diverted to fund the war effort, the state machinery is used as the prime enabler of violence and repression by the ruling clique against those who oppose it. In times of war, provision of electricity, water, gasoline, bread and other essential goods (in this case already hit by declining production and supply) inevitably becomes an instrument of power; the regime and, at times, rebel units have deployed these scarce resources so as to favour or punish specific groups.

Dynamics within the outer circles of the Assad regime are significant: the Ba'ath Party has 2.5m members whose loyalty and commitment have already eroded; salaries are paid to maintain the loyalty of the civil service, but many choose to remain home. Whether the tools of state can be revived during a post-Assad phase to provide security, services and a sense of national purpose would greatly depend on the political structure that emerges. With a strong and centralised government unlikely to emerge from the ruins of authoritarianism and civil war, only a dispensation of power that provides for decentralised administration alongside fair and representative parliamentary bodies stands a chance of instilling new life into the remnants of the Syrian state. Nearby countries provide examples of hybrid but arguably unfair and underperforming systems: Lebanon has a formal distribution of power among sects but no formalised decentralisation, while Iraq's constitution allows for regional devolution (as is the case with the Kurdistan Regional Government), without allotting positions to sects.

The influence of the various armed groups on the possible political outcomes is difficult to ascertain. The main brigades certainly have the power to frustrate or derail any political settlement that contradicts their interests or ideology, which considerably reduces the NC's room for manoeuvre. At the same time, these groups have, so far, been unable to impose their own political preferences on the rest of Syrian society. The rise of JN and other radical Islamist factions has the primary effect of framing political discourse around the place of political Islam, and may well force more moderate groups to harden their views. Other powerful armed factions, like Farouq, Tawheed and Ahfad al-Rasul, have yet to elaborate sophisticated political visions; they are more likely to defend their local interests while collaborating with political groups like the MB or new coalitions for nationwide debates.

The opposition's challenges

By early 2013, the NC's dilemmas had come into even sharper focus. With meagre resources and inconsistent foreign support, it could not establish and sustain a political presence inside Syria to shore-up its legitimacy or address the mounting humanitarian crisis. To extend the necessary backing and funding, its foreign supporters have required it to demonstrate an ability to unite and moderate the internal opposition, including autonomous rebel groups. Expectations of significant military aid following the formation of the SMC had not materialised, endangering its credibility with the very groups that it was supposed to coordinate. Among the political failures of the Syrian opposition, the inability to meaningfully appeal to pivotal social and confessional groups, with convincing guarantees, continues to loom large.

A key challenge for the Syrian opposition has been to unite and coordinate the military operations of the various rebel units through the SMC, led by Salim Idriss. As the conflict has grown in magnitude and complexity, more armed actors are pursuing autonomous agendas at odds with the objective of a unified and democratic Syria. Indeed, the political opposition remains at best marginal for the military behaviour of the overwhelming majority of armed groups. This state of affairs impedes its capacity to administer liberated areas, to provide credible guarantees to fence-sitting individuals, to engage in diplomatic talks and to design a viable political framework for a transition.

A recognition has emerged among senior opposition leaders that game-changing tactics are needed. The first was Moaz al-Khatib's announcement, in February 2013, that he was ready to enter direct but conditional talks with the regime. This decision contradicted the NC's charter that precluded talks with the regime and alienated influential segments of the opposition that had not been consulted, especially the SNC and the MB. Differences within the Syrian political opposition about the merits and modalities of talks with the regime are profound. For many oppositionists, any talks would provide Assad undue legitimacy and offer him an opportunity to splinter the opposition. From al-Khatib's perspective, on the other hand, an offer of dialogue, which garnered support among many Syrian revolutionary activists, serves to expose the regime's inflexibility and shift the burden onto other actors. This move cemented al-Khatib's standing as an independent and principled leader, committed to alleviating the population's suffering.

The second was a tougher approach toward the NC's international partners. Al-Khatib made comments in which he denounced the indecision and duplicity of his allies and decried regional competition over Syria. This culminated in a bitter public denunciation of unfulfilled promises of support and international indifference towards the Syrian conflict and a decision to boycott a Friends of Syria meeting in February 2013, later reversed after intense US and Gulf pressure.

Third is the controversial debate over the formation of a provisional government to administer liberated areas. The benefits would be significant should it obtain international *legal* recognition (that gave it the Syrian seats at the Arab League and the UN), as this would enable it to request international and UN-endorsed action and access to frozen Syrian assets abroad. It would also remove legal obstacles to financial and military bilateral support from other states. Rebel units under its umbrella would benefit from a legal status as the armed forces of Syria's legitimate government. Finally, such a government could begin developing institutional governance capacity, administer liberated Syrian territory, and formulate a transition platform that would address issues of transitional justice and political and security reform. It could also provide the opportunity for it to demonstrate its commitment to political and religious pluralism, through a civilian cabinet of competent politicians and techno-crats that would include defectors from the Assad regime.

However, the failure to obtain such recognition would damage the credibility of the NC inside Syria and boost the regime, psychologically and politically. Such a humiliation would further weaken the NC's authority over rebel forces, and its ability to moderate their most radical elements, and would also increase the dependency of the opposition on regional actors. Even if it did obtain this sought-after recognition, the risk that it would appear powerless and irrelevant to local suffer-ing would persist if adequate resources were not forthcoming. Finally, it would complicate al-Khatib's stated desire to engage in a dialogue with the regime under the right circumstances, but also the, arguably moribund, diplomatic efforts of Brahimi.

The ambivalent attitude of several Western states means that reservations over recognition should be taken seriously. While France and the UK encourage this step, the US remains recalci-trant, prioritising political cohesiveness, on-the-ground presence and delivery of services.

The regime's survival strategy

Judging from his own pronouncements and the regime's strategy, Assad takes comfort from having defied predictions of an inevitable and fast demise.[3] By January 2013, Assad had given six speeches extolling the resistance of his army and prom-ising imminent victories. Indeed, barring any significant policy change in Western capitals or new dynamics that would re-order power and calculations within the opaque ruling clique, the regime appears able to survive in the medium term.

Politically, the radicalisation of significant segments of the opposition and the escalating costs of the civil war have driven large numbers of Syrians into survival mode and noninvolve-ment while amplifying support within groups loyal to the regime or organically linked to its fate. In regime circles, the calculation prevails that a military stalemate, rebel fragmentation and policy paralysis abroad create conditions conducive to survival until at least 2014, a year in which a presidential election is scheduled to take place.[4] The regime's ability to hang on as the uprising continues to radicalise would also allow the narrative in the West to shift from romantic attachment to the revolutionary cause towards further alarm over the rise of Salafi-jihadism.

Even as its overall strength erodes, Assad's state remains the superior power, relative to the fragmented rebel front. Having defined more realistic military objectives, its forces can withstand armed pressure in areas deemed vital and amass firepower where needed. Tellingly, the rate and quality of military defections slowed in the second half of 2012. This has left the regime with a more reliable, deployable and hardened security core, while it expands its fighting capabilities through a network of less-costly militias, the National Defence Force and the Popular Committees.

How much of the military could be salvaged in a post-Assad set-up, given its implication in massive violence and its substantial internal erosion, remains uncertain. It is telling though that a key point of controversy within the Syrian opposition relates to the scope and manner of the reform of the security sector. This debate hinges, in particular, on the issue of guarantees to groups and individuals who may be open to loyalty shifts. As instruments of regime control and repression, the military, security services and the Ba'ath Party are already subject to calls for accountability.

The lesson of Iraq, where both the ruling party and security establishment were dissolved and their top ranks shunned at great cost, is that delicate management of accountability and reconciliation is a necessary condition for the rebuilding of the state. Many in the opposition are calling for a complete reorganisation of the security services and the prosecution of all senior figures, while others have adopted a more pragmatic line that would exclude only the most senior leadership.

A key test of the resilience of the regime will be its capacity to defend Damascus,[5] and holding the capital will be key to Assad's political standing. Although the regime's top circle itself shows no sign of fracturing, a long siege or the capture of Damascus could prompt regime elements to abandon Assad either to strike deals with the rebels or to seek protection with other power-brokers. If Damascus were lost, it is unlikely that the regime's command-and-control structure could endure in ways that would ensure a military presence outside the Alawite-dominated coastal areas. On the other hand, fending off an assault on the capital would likely result in greater rebel fragmentation and political disorientation within the opposition. The regime's political message would benefit from the repetition in Damascus of the grave shortcomings and mistakes of the rebel forces in Aleppo, and subsequent rise of jihadi factions. It would allow it to bolster its message that it is the sole viable administrator and guarantor against Islamic extremism, to both domestic and foreign audiences.

Signs that Assad has prepared a strong defence of the capital abound. Its control is a central organising principle of the regime since 1970, with military garrisons and loyalist neighbourhoods encircling the capital to keep potential dissenters in check. The deployment in the city of the regime's elite units and much of its artillery and air power, supplemented by newly created auxiliary forces, augurs a bloody and fierce battle. The military also occupies the high ground, especially Mount Qassioun on which the presidential palace sits. Neighbourhoods sympathetic to the rebels have been cleared or besieged, as in Daraya, which is close to a key military airport, or the restive towns of the Eastern Ghouta, which are constantly pummelled. Given the city's importance for both sides, the stakes are high and the fight for Damascus will likely be many times more bloody and costly than the one for Aleppo.

Were Damascus, and other key cities, to be lost, the possibility of a strategic retreat to the northwest, Alawite-dominated coastal region has gained prominence among analysts. (This is based on the, albeit short-lived, precedent of a quasi-autonomous Alawite political entity under the French mandate in the 1920s and 1930s.) The fierce fighting and massacres inside and on the outer ridge of this area, the return of many Alawite families to their villages and the communal mobilisation lend credence to the notion of a concerted regime strategy to that effect. Such a haven would benefit from adequate infrastructure (including seaports and airports) and a defensible rugged terrain on its eastern border. Sympathetic communities in bordering Turkey and, more importantly, Lebanon could provide goods and resources as well as arguably imperfect strategic depth. The regime would be able to move its remaining military forces and WMD arsenal there to provide for its defence and continued strategic relevance. It might also be able to count on members of other minorities, as well as sympathetic Sunnis, for support. Many Christians for example would prefer to live under Alawite protection that guarantees freedom of religion than under dreaded Islamist domination.

However, there are questions about the sustainability of an Alawite statelet. The incorporated territories contain large numbers of non-Alawite citizens, who may not, in fact, be sympathetic to this new political entity. From the regime's perspective then, securing the area may well require sectarian cleansing. The coastal region does not grow enough food or have energy resources to support its population and a militia engaged in an ongoing civil war. It would be vulnerable to a blockade and would have no bordering state ally, and would require substantive and continuous foreign support, from military supplies to gasoline and funding. Much would depend on how Iraq, Russia and especially Iran would evaluate the strategic worth of such an entity and the cost of maintaining its existence.

Notably, the establishment of an Alawite enclave would fracture Syria and exacerbate the ongoing process of territorial and political disintegration. It would also deprive any new Syrian government of access to the sea and pose significant threat to its control of the hinterland.

The diplomatic solution: delusion or only game in town?

Besides humanitarian and geopolitical considerations, a driving principle of UN diplomacy and Western policy in encouraging a negotiated transition is the belief that doing so would preserve the key pillars of the Syrian state and facilitate post-Assad reconciliation and reconstruction. (Of course, the extent to which the instruments of state could be revived to provide security, services and a sense of national purpose would greatly depend on the political structure that emerges.)

The search for a negotiated settlement continues to face significant obstacles. To succeed, it needs to engage and reconcile the views of players at three levels: global, regional and local. At each level, and with ascending difficulty, structural and political barriers prevent a rapprochement in the medium term.

The strategy of Brahimi in the last months of 2012 has been to bridge differences between the US and Russia in the hope that they would be able to pressure their own regional and local allies into a negotiation. The views of these two global powers on Syria are closer than those of regional and local actors. Both agree on the need for a negotiated solution that involves the Assad regime, but differ over the form this would take and how to address the fate of Assad. A weakness in Brahimi's strategy is the assumption that both the US and Russia have not only the will but also the ability to pressure their regional and Syrian allies. In fact, US dithering has cost Washington goodwill and leverage among both the opposition and the rebels, while Russian leverage over Assad remains untested and uncertain.

At the regional level, the competition between the various players has only intensified as respective Iranian and Gulf support for Assad and the rebels has increased. The decoupling of the diplomatic track from their policies inside Syria suggests that diplomacy amounts to little more than a formality. For its part, Turkey has been anxious to contain the regional repercussions of the crisis for fear that it would further poison its already deteriorating relations with Iran and Iraq and feed the perception that it has been conducting a sectarian foreign policy.

At the local level, both sides have remained primarily invested in the armed struggle. Assad used his January 2013 speech to reaffirm his uncompromising position: a dialogue would only happen on his terms and after his opponents surrendered their weapons. Using the ambiguity in the Geneva plan over the transition and his own fate, Assad announced a process of reforms and polls that would occupy the political scene until 2014, the year scheduled for presidential elections. In later weeks, Syrian officials continued to outline the conditions under which dialogue would take place, while Foreign Minister Walid Muallem described any discussion of the fate of Assad to be 'unacceptable'.[6]

The troubled regional picture

The repercussions of Syria's crisis outside its borders have been far-reaching, direct and destabilising. In less than two years, its regional impact has surpassed that of Iraq's US-induced civil war. A mix of factors had contained Iraq's conflict and prevented regional contagion – in particular, its centrality in US policy and the US military presence in Iraqi internal dynamics regulated regional interference until 2010.

In comparison, the struggle over Syria has drawn in and spilled out into every bordering state. Despite significant military and political risks, neighbouring states and regional non-state actors have mobilised significant resources and intervened, directly and overtly. Unlike in Iraq, where the new political realities were (begrudgingly) accepted by its neighbours, the conflict in Syria has produced ever-hardening positions about the Assad regime pitting regional powers against each other. For Turkey, it has had direct security implications and its outcome could make or break Ankara's regional ambitions; for Iran, it has determined the level and nature of its influence in the Levant; for the Gulf states, it has amounted to a unique opportunity to achieve extensive strategic and political goals. By early 2012, these states, each having set clear objectives and dedicated significant resources to achieving them, were locked in a zero-sum regional game and had little room for diplomatic manoeuvre. Notably, a lack of US leadership, as it hesitated about the appropriate level of its involvement, resulted in ambiguity and contributed to the intensification of regional competition (between Saudi Arabia and Qatar for example), in a significantly more fluid environment.

By early 2013, the territories of Iraq, Turkey, Jordan, Lebanon and Israel had all been affected in myriad ways, from refugee inflows to cross-border incidents. Their regular militaries and intelligence services had been engaged in Syria-related operations and had developed contingency plans. The regime itself had also actively sought to implicate its regional allies, while raising the costs of intervention for its foes. In a sense, Lebanon's and Iraq's geography and links to Syria made entanglement inevitable and aggravated internal divides. Both Assad and the rebels view these countries as part of the geography of the conflict. For Assad, preventing Lebanon's Sunnis from boosting the rebellion and protecting key centres inside Syria required securing the Lebanese border, with the help of Hizbullah, and similar considerations have set relations with Iraq. For the rebels, developing strategic depth, supply lines and conduits for incoming fighters necessitated a strong presence in each of Syria's neighbours.

Given the profound political and societal fragmentation, it is unsure what kind of political landscape will emerge should a weakened Assad survive, or should he be ousted. While he remains the focal point of the opposition, local dynamics continue to shape and define the conflict more than national trends – it is local imperatives that drive the calculations of both armed groups and civilian activists. As funding from Syrian individuals and expatriates declines due to fatigue and the length of the conflict, battalions have to either pool resources or seek new funders. Groups also struggle to define the scope of their activity: some prefer to stick to local self-defence, while others have more ambitious goals. For example, the weakening of the locally-recruited Shuhada Suriya in Jabal al-Zawiyah has benefitted Islamist factions. Crucially, a greater differentiation between the various fronts is also perceptible. Rebel commanders find it difficult to coordinate operations, let alone inject political and strategic coherence. While Turkey and Qatar are heavily invested in the west and north, Saudi Arabia has focused its efforts on the south and the east.

The objective of ousting Assad is a powerful glue binding Syria's various opposition movements together, but it may not survive the worsening of the conflict, while achievement of this goal may serve only to begin a new phase of competition between the various factions. Assad's weakening and the hardships of war have opened up opportunities for the expression of long-repressed, as well as new, local and communal loyalties. These may be destined to clash over resources, territory and ideology. It is possible that Assad himself could endure as one, and possibly the strongest, of Syria's warlords, while his ouster could give rise to one or more Alawite chieftains in his place. Such dynamics, if not properly managed by the political opposition, could usher in warlordism across the country, engender state failure and allow radical jihadi groups to operate freely – thus creating a situation with similarities to that of Somalia in the past two decades.

If it were to happen, the demise of the Assad regime would probably be only the end of the first phase of a deeper political transformation that would test national and societal cohesion even further. As crucial will be the manner of such a fall: if not accompanied by regionally-sponsored political negotiations between the various warring factions, Syria's current divisions may well sharpen and crystallise. Much would depend on the dispensation of power: who holds power inside the opposition but also inside the regime as it unravels. Political and security chaos in Damascus would only facilitate disintegration elsewhere and weaken further already tenuous national bonds.

A more optimistic outcome would be the competent management of the various centrifugal forces pulling Syrian society apart (the Kurds in the northeast, the Alawites in the northwest, plus other expressions of regionalism) that culminates into a power-sharing arrangement with willing remnants of the Assad regime. The substance of such an arrangement would have to recognise the primacy of citizenship over other forms of identity and establish an inclusive form of government that secures minority rights alongside greater political participation. Syrians derive great pride from the role that non-Sunnis have played in the formation of the modern Syrian state, including the Christian statesman Fares el-Khouri, and from Syria's brief if turbulent experiment with parliamentary democracy in the 1940s and 1950s. Such precedents don't amount to a guarantee of success, but the capacity of the emerging Syrian leadership to root its political action in the country's arguably short-lived happier past could help it to navigate what will prove, no matter what, to be a stormy transition.

Notes

1   'Socioeconomic Roots and Impact of the Syrian Crisis', Syrian Center for Policy Research, January 2013, http://www.scpr-syria.org/tmpPreLaunch/SyrianCrisisReportEN.pdf.

2   Zalewski, 'Syria's Rebel Judges Promise Sharia With Justice', *Time*, 10 August 2012, http://world.time.com/2012/08/10/syrias-rebel-judges-promise-sharia-justice-with-mercy/.

3   Hokayem, 'No Surrender', *Foreign Policy*, 7 January 2013, http://www.foreignpolicy.com/articles/2013/01/07/no_surrender.

4   *Ibid.*

5   Hokayem, 'Syria's Battle Royale', *Foreign Policy*, 11 February 2013, http://www.foreignpolicy.com/articles/2013/02/11/syria_s_battle_royale.

6   'Syria crisis: Foreign Minister Muallem calls for talks', *BBC News*, 20 January 2013, http://www.bbc.co.uk/news/world-middle-east-21106163.

Adelphi books are published eight times a year by Routledge Journals, an imprint of Taylor & Francis, 4 Park Square, Milton Park, Abingdon, Oxfordshire OX14 4RN, UK.

A subscription to the institution print edition, ISSN 1944-5571, includes free access for any number of concurrent users across a local area network to the online edition, ISSN 1944-558X. Taylor & Francis has a flexible approach to subscriptions enabling us to match individual libraries' requirements. This journal is available via a traditional institutional subscription (either print with free online access, or online-only at a discount) or as part of the Strategic, Defence and Security Studies subject package or Strategic, Defence and Security Studies full text package. For more information on our sales packages please visit www.tandfonline.com/librarians_pricinginfo_journals.

2013 Annual Adelphi Subscription Rates			
Institution	£557	$979 USD	€824
Individual	£199	$338 USD	€270
Online only	£487	$857 USD	€721

Dollar rates apply to subscribers outside Europe. Euro rates apply to all subscribers in Europe except the UK and the Republic of Ireland where the pound sterling price applies. All subscriptions are payable in advance and all rates include postage. Journals are sent by air to the USA, Canada, Mexico, India, Japan and Australasia. Subscriptions are entered on an annual basis, i.e. January to December. Payment may be made by sterling cheque, dollar cheque, international money order, National Giro, or credit card (Amex, Visa, Mastercard).

For a complete and up-to-date guide to Taylor & Francis journals and books publishing programmes, and details of advertising in our journals, visit our website: http://www.tandfonline.com.

Ordering information:
USA/Canada: Taylor & Francis Inc., Journals Department, 325 Chestnut Street, 8th Floor, Philadelphia, PA 19106, USA. UK/Europe/Rest of World: Routledge Journals, T&F Customer Services, T&F Informa UK Ltd., Sheepen Place, Colchester, Essex, CO3 3LP, UK.

Advertising enquiries to:
USA/Canada: The Advertising Manager, Taylor & Francis Inc., 325 Chestnut Street, 8th Floor, Philadelphia, PA 19106, USA. Tel: +1 (800) 354 1420. Fax: +1 (215) 625 2940. UK/Europe/Rest of World: The Advertising Manager, Routledge Journals, Taylor & Francis, 4 Park Square, Milton Park, Abingdon, Oxfordshire OX14 4RN, UK. Tel: +44 (0) 20 7017 6000. Fax: +44 (0) 20 7017 6336.

The print edition of this journal is printed on ANSI conforming acid-free paper by Bell & Bain, Glasgow, UK.